Rinker on Collectibles

Rinker on Collectibles

Harry L. Rinker

Wallace-Homestead Book Company
Radnor, Pennsylvania

Published in Radnor, Pennsylvania 19089, by Wallace-Homestead Book Company

Designed by Anthony Jacobson
Illustrations by Frank Hill

Library of Congress Cataloging-in-Publication Data
Rinker, Harry L.
Rinker on collectibles / Harry L. Rinker.
p. cm.
Essays originally published in the author's syndicated column.
Includes index.
ISBN 0-87069-526-6
1. Collectibles—Miscellanea. 2. Collectors and collecting—Miscellanea. I. Title.
AM231.R54 1989
790.1'32—dc 19 88-51502
CIP

Manufactured in the United States of America

1 2 3 4 5 6 7 8 9 0 8 7 6 5 4 3 2 1 0 9

to

Harry L. Rinker, Jr.

In D. F. Jones's *Colossus*, an anticomputer science-fiction novel, the defense of the entire free world is turned over to Colossus, a supercomputer that will be the sole arbiter of war and peace. When the computer is activated, it types out a five-word message that I consider one of the most frightening lines ever written in science fiction:

"Flash, there is another mechanism."

Harry Junior inherited my accumulating gene. Watch out world.

"There is another."

Contents

Preface

COLLECTIBLES have always gotten short shrift from antiques collectors. It finally ticked me off. The result was "Rinker on Collectibles."

"Rinker on Collectibles" began with a twofold purpose: (1) to sing the glories of the twentieth-century, mass-produced, inexpensive collectible and (2) to elevate collectibles to the same level of respectability as antiques. As "Rinker on Collectibles" evolved, a third purpose arose: to speculate on how the collectibles field functions and what motivates the collectibles collector.

When I formulated the concept for "Rinker on Collectibles" 2½ years ago, I carefully examined the weekly columns in the antiques and collectibles field. Most columns used a question-and-answer format. A few contained an introductory paragraph or two about some object or category. Only one contained full-text columns examining an idea or collecting category in depth, and that one concentrated primarily on antiques.

I decided "Rinker on Collectibles" would alternate weekly between a question-and-answer column and a text column, the latter consisting of two types: (1) factual columns and (2) opinion columns. It is the opinion columns that I think make "Rinker on Collectibles" truly unique.

Most antiques and collectibles columns deal only with the positive, glittering side of the business. There are millions of hidden treasures waiting to be found with a minimum of hard work; everyone in the business is honest. Horse feathers!

I like to think of myself as one of the nation's cheerleaders for antiques and collectibles. But, I am a realistic cheerleader. The truth comes first—good, bad, or indifferent. It is time to demystify antiques and collectibles and subject the field to some hard analysis.

Several of the opinion columns from "Rinker on Collectibles" have evoked pointed criticism. Hurray—they were meant to do that. The opinion columns are designed to make readers think. They are not the gospel according to Harry.

"Rinker on Collectibles" was removed from *Antiques & Auction News*, the trade paper in which the column started, because it was too controversial. I was flattered.

I am not asking you to agree with all that I write. But I am asking you to *think* about what I write. Ponder the points. If you think your ideas are better, drop me a line and argue your case. I am willing to change my opinion if your argument is better than mine. Are you prepared to do the same?

During the past year, I have received a wealth of letters from individuals who have missed one or more of the text columns. Would I please send them a copy? This book is a response to these requests.

From the start, I envisioned a time when the text columns from "Rinker on Collectibles" would be compiled into book form. Here is the method of organization that I think provides a level of continuity to the presentation:

☞ *Introduction.* After defining a collectible, I will discuss why the collectibles market is the most vital and viable portion of today's antiques market.

☞ *Market Consideration.* Details a series of general rules and philosophies that govern the workings of the collectibles market.

☞ *What You Need to Know About Pricing.* Because of the *recent* nature of collectibles, the rules used to value antiques do not necessarily apply. Read this section and you will take the first steps to becoming a true insider in the collectibles market.

☞ *Understanding the Collector.* Explores the things that make the collectibles collector very different from the antiques collector. *Vive la differénce.*

☞ *Research and Catalog Hints.* Some basic things you need to know about doing research and cataloging collectibles.

☞ *Sources of Supply.* Some thoughts on where collectibles can be bought and sold.

☞ *Collectible Categories.* Twenty collecting categories that have been singled out for special attention.

☞ *Weird and Strange Things People Collect.* I had to leave out some categories for fear of censorship. You will be delighted with what remains.

☞ *The Future.* A new collecting era is about to dawn. Some advance warning of what's to come.

While the columns that I have assembled for this book are a self-contained unit, they are not my final word on the subject of collectibles. "Rinker on Collectibles" will continue to appear in the years ahead. Now that you have caught up on what you missed, I hope you will follow the column into the future.

Acknowledgments

CINDY Engle from *Joel Sater's Antiques & Auction News* was the person who encouraged me to begin writing this column. The name of the paper has been changed, Cindy is no longer with them, and they dropped my column. But the column continues to survive and grow, both in scope and circulation. Thanks, Cindy, for the initial vote of confidence.

Diane Stoneback, Home and Food Editor for *The Morning Call*, Allentown, Pennsylvania, is responsible for the expansion of "Rinker on Collectibles" to the daily newspaper market. Her patience and support are tested monthly as columns continue to reach her just before deadline. After 2½ years, we are still civil to each other. It says more about her character than mine.

Connie Moore, my wife, continues to remain married to me no matter what I write about her and her family in my columns. She has never forced me to edit a column even when she has read it before publication. I thank her for her resilience.

Most of my readers are used to seeing Ellen L. Schroy's name on the masthead of the Warman price guides. No matter what title she has there, you should understand that she carries another in my heart: friend. I have watched Ellen's love and knowledge of antiques and collectibles grow over the past seven years. Initially, I was her teacher. Now I am not certain who teaches whom.

Terese J. Oswald, Brenda Verderosa, and Myra Goldfarb, present and past employees in my many business enterprises, have all contributed to the success of "Rinker on Collectibles." Likewise, a special thanks to the many publishers and editors who have selected "Rinker on Collectibles" for inclusion in their newspapers and magazines.

Finally, my thanks to all the collectors, dealers, and reference librarians across the country who took the time to research and answer the questions I raised. This book is a tribute to their generosity.

Harry L. Rinker
Rinker Enterprises
P.O. Box 248
Zionsville, PA 18092

Part 1
Introduction

Hello, Young Lovers, Wherever You Are

I like antiques, but I love collectibles. Since I make my living writing about both, I suppose I should not express a preference for one over the other. However, I am tired of hearing that collectibles are second-rate or that they are just junk.

The collectibles market and the antiques market are not two separate entities. They are one and the same. If an antique is something that is classified as one hundred years old, then by this definition alone we have only eleven more years to wait until we have our first twentieth-century antique.

Try telling someone who collects mechanical banks or Art Deco that they are not collecting antiques. Plenty of twentieth-century items are considered antiques by dealers and collectors with little or no second thoughts. American art pottery is a good example.

In reality the only real differentiating line between an antique and a collectible is price. If it costs above $1,000, it is generally viewed as an antique. If it costs below $250, it is a collectible. It's a tossup for objects in the $250 to $1,000 range.

Collectibles are merely a part of the greater antiques market, just as Orientalia or European porcelains are part of that market. One of my purposes here is to convince auctioneers, dealers, and collectors to take the collectibles portion of the market seriously.

The truth is that grandma and grandpa's attic in today's world does not contain early American furniture or even Civil War memorabilia. It contains twentieth-century items. Heck, my grandchild pokes around in a grandpa's attic that contains Disneyana, Boy Scout items, penny arcade cards, and Hopalong Cassidy stuff.

When I speak to auctioneer or dealer groups, I am amazed at how few know anything about the collectibles market. It is almost as though they consider themselves too good to handle collectibles. The collectibles market is as sophisticated as the upscale portion of the antiques market. In fact, I think it is better organized and has far more selling and buying vehicles than its more expensive counterpart.

Since so few understand the collectibles market, I have decided to write about collectibles, and only collectibles. You won't find any information here about Chippendale furniture, Meissen porcelain, or Tiffany silver. What you will find is plenty of facts about the mass-produced items of the twentieth century that constitute so much of the childhood of our children, ourselves, and our parents.

It's easy to identify a collectible. Take an object and ask yourself if it fits three or more of the following criteria: mass-produced, made after 1900, made in America, collected in America (no European would be caught dead with a collection of Avon bottles), and the majority of similar items in the same category sell between 50¢ and $200. In fact, if your item fits just two of these criteria, chances are it is a collectible.

Why am I in love with collectibles? First and foremost, it's the people. People who collect collectibles are enthusiastic and vital. Equally important, they are fanatics.

Honestly, I do not know a more abnormal group than the collectibles collectors. They are possessed—possessed with having fun, learning about what they own, and exchanging that information with anyone who is willing to listen. I think the average collectibles collector knows far more about his or her objects than does the average antiques collector.

Second, collectibles are affordable. You can actually assemble a good beginning collection in almost every collectible category for between $500 and $1,000. Even a person on an extremely limited budget can find something to buy, possess, and love. There are no million-dollar tilt-top tables in the collectibles field.

Third, collectibles are a wonderful justification for adults continuing to play with the things they enjoyed as children. Let's face it! It's more fun to play with the goodies than having them sit in a china cabinet, on a shelf, or in a box stored under the bed. In most cases, if a piece is damaged, you can always buy another one.

Nostalgia is one of the biggest draws in the collectibles field. I collect Hopalong Cassidy memorabilia, not Roy Rogers or Gene Autry memorabilia, because Hoppy was and still is my cowboy hero. Collectibles allow you to be proud of your youth. You are helping make all those things your parents thought were so dumb part of history.

Roll out those Barbie dolls, the high school letter sweaters, and the ill-fitting uniforms from your World War II or Korean War service. In today's world, it's all collectible.

Sometimes this column will be serious and factual. Whenever possible, I'll try to throw in a touch of humor. Each column will give you some information that you can use to advantage in your business or collecting interests.

My remarks will be opinionated and occasionally controversial. I may like antiques and love collectibles, but I do not worship them. I have developed a reputation over the years for saying what I think regardless of the consequences. You won't always agree with my version of the truth.

The one thing I do promise is that I will do my best not to be dull. We have more than enough boring columns about antiques now.

Today's collectibles are tomorrow's antiques. Read on, and I'll prove it.

Grandma's Attic

HAVE you thought about grandmother's attic recently? Antiquers and collectors still dream of attics filled with objects from our colonial and federal past: Chippendale highboys, documents signed by presidents, paintings by Stuart and Copley, Chinese export and Meissen porcelains. They even will settle for a few choice pieces from the Civil War era.

For the pioneer American antiques collectors at the end of the nineteenth century, this vision was reality. But, now, it is one hundred years later. Grandmother's attic is not what it used to be. It's time to change our thinking.

I'm a grandfather. My attic is not filled with nineteenth-century antiques. It is crammed with Boy Scout material, arcade cards, Hopalong Cassidy items, 45 rpm records, Disneyana, and other memorabilia that someone who grew up in the 1950s would save. The attic of my grandparents contained a few objects from the nineteenth century, but far more goodies from the period of World War I through the 1940s.

Let's face it. Grandma's attic is a twentieth-century attic. If a collector or dealer accepts this rather monumental fact, he or she needs to develop a whole new set of values in the antiques and collectibles field.

The antiques purist has always viewed 1830 as the magic date at which objects ceased to be antiques and no longer were worthy of veneration. Winterthur, a trend-setting, elitist museum, has advanced the date into the 1850s. Others rely on the hundred-year rule, supplied to us by the Custom Service of our government. You do not pay duty on an object imported into the United States that is over one hundred years old because it is an "antique."

I think there is a simpler way to define an antique. An antique is something that belonged to one's grandparents or great-grandparents and now is old enough to be considered a family heirloom. Grandparents are not part of the present. They are part of the past. As founts of wisdom and understanding, they represent what has gone before, not what is about to be. They are old, their things are old.

Now, I must confess that I am very uncomfortable with this line of reasoning. Even though I am a grandparent, I do not feel old. However, whenever I mention in one of my classes that I used to ride the trolley from Hellertown to Bethlehem (Pennsylvania) to attend the weekly model-railroader meetings at the YMCA, and then objectively study the look on my audiences' faces, I realize that I am old, like it or not.

For each of us, there appears to be a point at which something becomes old. For me, it is World War II. I think it has something to do with conscious memory. I do not have very vivid memories of World War II. The Korean War and the first Eisenhower election are the events that made me aware of historical time.

How many living individuals do you know who were born before 1900? How about before 1915? For most of the adults living today, their vision of what is old begins only as early as the 1920s and in many cases is not earlier than the 1940s and 1950s.

Established antiques dealers traditionally have scorned anything from the twentieth century. If they want to stay in business and appeal to their customers, they are going to have to change. They have allowed Art Nouveau and Art Deco items to creep into their shops. The modernist movement of the mid-twentieth century is next. So are twentieth-century collectibles.

When I began compiling material for collectibles books, I promised myself that I would not be shocked by changing prices. My job is to report prices and keep myself neutral. Well, in addition to being a reporter, I am also a collector. When I have to pay money out of my own pocket, I am shocked.

Nothing brought this home to me more than my recent acquisition of some Hopalong Cassidy memorabilia through Ted Hake's Americana & Collectibles mail auction. The auction takes place through the mail. However, on the last day, you have the right to call up, check your bids, and make whatever raises you deem appropriate. The auction is over when "ten minutes pass without a call." The auction was to conclude late Wednesday evening.

At 5:50 A.M. on Thursday morning, I got up early to make the call to check my bids. I expected the auction would be over. It was still going strong. It lasted until mid-morning.

One of the items on which I was bidding was a Hopalong Cassidy vinyl shoe holder. It had jumped from $60 early Wednesday evening to over $120 on Thursday morning. The next bid had to exceed $138 to secure the object. A 1950 shoe holder at $120 plus! Have we all gone mad?

The twentieth-century "collectible" is about to become a thing of the past. Too many twentieth-century items are now becoming viewed as antiques by collectors. This is caused in part by age and in part by price level. If you are going to pay hundreds of dollars for an object, it had better be an antique, not a collectible.

The shock of recognition that grandma's attic is a twentieth-century repository is about to be compounded by the arrival of the twenty-first century. A mystical transformation is going to occur in our minds when the year 2000 rolls around. The very words "twentieth century" will come to denote an earlier time. The acceptance of what is considered antique will take a quantum leap forward.

As grandma's attic has been assuming its twentieth-century character, it faces a major crisis: it is disappearing. Many modern homes are being built without attics and basements. The millions of individuals who live in apartments have only closets and a limited amount of storage space in a basement. Grandma is becoming a "thrower-outer" and not a "saver." If grandma does not do it, who will save our historical past for us?

Part 2
Market Considerations

The Multifaceted Collectible

ONE of the things that fascinates me most about collectibles is that they rarely fit neatly into one collecting category.

The 1949 calendar from the Chesapeake and Ohio Railway features "Chessie" the cat sleeping on the floor while her two kittens play with an electric train set. The artist is Charles E. Bracker. This one collectible has six major potential buyers: the advertising character collector, the calendar collector, the cat collector, the illustrator collector, the railroad collector (also the specialized C & O collector), and the toy train collector. This list only scratches the surface. The book collector (books are illustrated), the collector of period-setting references (it clearly pictures a 1940s living room), and others could also be attracted to the calendar.

The next amazing realization is that each of these collectors is willing to pay a different price for the same object. A collectible does not have *a* price. It has several prices depending on who is doing the collecting. This is why each category in *Warman's Americana & Collectibles* is priced based on what the collector in that category will pay. It is why several objects appear in the book in more than one category with more than one price.

When dealers price a collectible, they should carefully consider their targeted market. The higher the price, the lower the number of potential buyers. Suppose a dealer bought the 1947 C & O calendar for $5. He would sell it in short order if he asked $10, thus doubling his money. Almost all the collector groups listed above would be willing buyers at this price. However, the top market price is $50 plus from the railroad collectors. If the dealer sets up at a railroad show, this is a good price. But, if no train collector is likely to come by his shop or booth, this price is far too high.

I was recently talking with Jeanne Bertoia, author of *Doorstops: Identification & Values* (Collector Books, 1985), about how collectors with other collecting interests do in bidding against collectors of doorstops. Doorstop collectors can still outbid the sports theme collectors and animal theme collectors for doorstops.

However, the Aunt Jemima and Black memorabilia collectors, Halloween collectors, Nursery Rhyme theme collectors, and Women's collectibles collectors usually will outbid the doorstop collectors.

But you don't have to go outside a category to find a complex hierarchy of pricing deviations. Assume you have a child's Hopalong Cassidy cowboy hat made by Bailey of Hollywood from the early 1950s. Within the cowboy collectibles category, the general collector, the Hoppy collector, the TV collector, and the B-movie collector all would be competing for the hat. Once again, each would be willing to pay a vastly different price for it.

What does all this mean about the stability of prices in the collectibles area? Well, simply put, prices are not stable. This is a fact of life that the collector of collectibles must accept.

In fact, many of the prices in the collectibles field are speculative. They also are heavily craze- and decorator-oriented. Collectors tend not to buy with the idea of selling. They usually expect to retain their collections forever. Since the entire collectibles field is relatively new, there is not a strongly established tradition in most categories of sale, resale, and continued resale. If I were approaching the question from an investment point of view, I certainly would concentrate on the antiques side of the field rather than the collectibles side.

But I love collectibles. Each week adds several more pieces to my hoard. Why? Because the multifaceted nature of the collectible gives me so many ways to enjoy it and such a wide variety of people also have a love affair with it. Some people call my home, office, and storage shed a junkyard. I won't tell you what my wife calls them. I think of them as buried treasure because I'm always discovering something I forgot I saved. *Macht nichts aus!*

When Does Something Become Collectible? Rinker's Thirty-Year Rule

For the first thirty years of anything's life,
all its value is speculative.

In spite of the suggestive claims of the Franklin Mint, Goebel, or the U.S. Historical Society, you cannot manufacture an instant collectible. Among the major modern collectible markets that have collapsed during the past decade are limited-edition whiskey bottles, Avon bottles, and, most recently, collector plates. A New Jersey dealer summed it up best, "Even Precious Moments are not precious anymore."

Perhaps one of the most startling examples of the roller coaster effect involved in the speculative fever attached to modern collectibles is illustrated by the 1971 Goebel Hummel Christmas plate entitled "Heavenly Angel." Originally issued in the $25 range, the plate was selling in the 1970s above $1,500, with some reports of prices in excess of $3,000.

I was offered close to $2,000 for the one I own. Only one word describes my refusing this offer: dumb.

Today the 1971 Hummel Christmas plate books for $700 to $800. But, show me a dealer who can command this price? In reality, the plate can be bought for between $500 and $600. For $1,500 most dealers would be happy to sell a collector the full set of Hummel Christmas plates issued between 1971 and 1986.

Further, if someone wanted to purchase the full set, I would suggest waiting. The collector plate market will continue to drop. It still has a long way to go before hitting bottom, despite several attempts by the Bradford Exchange to prop it up.

Rinker's Thirty-Year Rule applies and is very simple: For the first thirty years of anything's life, all its value is speculative.

It requires at least thirty years for several important events to transpire that are critical to the long-term value stability of any collectible object. First, a major portion of the production run (often millions of examples are made) needs to be destroyed by use, decay, or diligent mothers who clean their children's rooms and throw out stuff when their offspring go to college or get married.

Second, the individuals who grew up with the objects need to have grown old enough to miss them, nostalgic enough to want to reacquire them, and rich enough to afford them. The key to value stability in the collectible market is a fond, almost idyllic memory of the object sought. The market has to be continually tested. The same pieces must continue to reappear, and they must bring roughly the same price.

A key to remember in the collector plate market is that the manufacturers do not expect their product to be resold. They want them saved as keepsakes. When the vast majority are resold within ten years of manufacture, what happens? In general, they bring between one-third and one-half of the original selling price.

If this is true, why isn't this well known? Speculators and the Bradford Exchange fan the flames of hope by touting the few examples that have captured the collector's imagination and increased in value above the original purchase price. Speculators manipulate the market. Buyers must be aware.

But this strategy is destined to long-term failure. At first, collectors hoard. Manufacturers respond to the speculation by both increasing production runs and raising prices. Rival companies produce closely related products. As collectors buy at higher and higher prices and in greater and greater quantities (greed is a wonderful inducement), they get in deeper and deeper.

Trends change. The less-than-serious collectors begin to offer their collector plates for sale. Remember, they believe they will easily get more than they paid for them. The market is flooded. People slowly realize how many examples of the same object are really out there.

When the market turns downward, the devoted collectors are afraid to sell. For some reason there is a psychological barrier that prevents a collector or dealer from selling a piece at a loss. In summary, they are stuck.

If you stop and think about it, when has the American public maintained a thirty-year relationship with any decorating or collectible trend? The average American is conditioned to change, not stability. Buy, throw out, and buy again.

I do not mean to suggest that I make it a rule not to collect anything unless it is thirty years old. My house, office, garage, and shacks contain many items less than thirty years old. The key is the attitude I take when I acquire them.

If I have to buy them, I do so with my "mad" money. If the price seems fair, I pay it. Rarely do I pay more than a few dollars. I buy the objects because I like them, want to use them in my educational activities, or include them in my study collection. If they never achieve full collectible status and have to be discarded, so be it.

If you can collect modern material without allowing speculation to enter into the picture too much, you approach the real essence of the joy of collecting. I have a number of collections going with this approach, and I am having a ball.

What's in a Name?

WHILE making a deposit at my local branch bank recently, I glanced down at my bank money bag and saw the logo for the First National Bank of Allentown. I was horrified. I couldn't believe I was actually using an obsolete and potentially valuable collectible for everyday purposes. I was on the horns of a dilemma, torn between the advice I constantly give about living and using your collectibles and my instinct to stash away the bank money bag to prevent any further deterioration through use.

The name "First National Bank of Allentown" is now obsolete. The bank was swallowed up by Meridian Bank, a large corporate conglomerate, which retired the old name. I suppose there is some justice to all this. First National Bank was instrumental in seeing that the same thing happened to Saucon Valley Bank in Hellertown, Macungie Bank in Macungie, and several other banks in the Lehigh Valley region of Pennsylvania, where I live.

Mergers are a way of life today. Long-established traditional names are nonchalantly cast aside in favor of a new corporate identity. Remember when Exxon was Esso and USX was U.S. Steel? Several public-relations firms specialize in finding new names for companies. I don't know whether to thank them or curse them.

Each time a name changes, anything containing the old name becomes immediately collectible. Collectors frequently take years to recognize this fact. While the loss is immediate, the memory of the old institution lingers for at least one or two generations.

When I was born, the principal downtown department store in Bethlehem was Bush and Bull. When I was a teenager, the store changed its name to Orr's. I still hear old-time Bethlehemites say they are going shopping at Bush and Bull. I do it myself.

Connie, my wife, is constantly frustrated with me over two words that I simply cannot seem to purge from my vocabulary: icebox and pop. I constantly inquire, "What's in the icebox to eat?" The word "refrigerator" has no reality to me. When the girl at Roy Rogers asks me what I want to drink, my usual reply is "a pop." The startled look on the teenager's face tells me that I have failed a test in modern communication once again. I think everyone has some obsolete words in their vocabulary that are simply too ingrained to give up.

Years ago, your local post office canceled all the mail it received. Today, it goes to regional postal centers. Unless I request a local cancellation when I mail a letter in Zionsville, it is stamped Lehigh Valley. There are people who collect obsolete postmarks. Whenever I examine a postcard collection, I always look at the postmarks before I look at the front of the cards. The postmark on a card may be more valuable than the picture on the front.

What many people do not realize is that the trend to eliminate old names has a rather sinister side. It is the destruction of localism, the homogenization of America. National corporations want national identities. Regional institutions want a name with which everyone can identify. They simply do not want a local name as part of their title. What kind of a name is First Valley Bank? Where is the First Valley? Is there a Second Valley or a Third Valley? The answer is no. First Valley is a meaningless corporate name without any regional identity whatsoever.

Last weekend I attended an antiques and collectibles show and watched a growing number of young collectors buying scraps of the past that contained obsolete local names. Among the new possessions of these collectors were ashtrays, calendar plates, clipboard clips, employee identification tags, and promotional giveaways with logos, all bespeaking a long-lost era when there was such a thing as "local" and "company" pride. At least a few out there are saving some of this history.

What happened to all the advertising signs, stationery, giveaway premiums, and other items that had the name or logo of First National Bank of Allentown? Corporate headquarters issued orders to throw them out. I requested a few examples for my personal collection of local items with obsolete names. The bank refused. *[Note: The bank reconsidered after this article appeared, and my collection is now rich in First National Bank of Allentown material.]*

However, not everyone at the bank is so disparaging of the past. I know a few old-timers who carefully put some examples aside in the hope that some small part of the past would be preserved.

I heard through the grapevine that there is a secret hoard of First National Bank of Allentown labeled items in a basement somewhere in the Allentown area. Rumor has it that Meridian is going to hold a tag sale of bank items, open only to their employees, with the profits going to a local charity. After they read this column and find that the items are now collectibles and should increase in value in the years ahead, they might want to think again and hang onto them for awhile. It is rather ironic that they have money in the bank and don't even realize it.

We need a "Save the Old Name Society" that will rise up in rightful indignation when someone threatens to change a perfectly good old name. They will not win every battle, but they might win a few.

"What's in a name? That which we call a rose by any other name would smell as sweet."—William Shakespeare, *Romeo and Juliet,* Act 2, Scene 2, Line 43. Meridian and a lot of other big corporations hope this holds true. Good luck!

Rinker's Rule of Ten

I must confess that I am no longer amazed at what people collect. Truly, there is a collector for everything. Recently I joined the ranks of the toilet paper, laxative tins and boxes, church bazaar items, and false-teeth collectors. My staff is keeping a list of the totally weird categories that I collect. When the number reaches a hundred, they plan to commit me. I think their list already has more than eighty categories of items on it.

But, is everything collectible? Previously I would not have hesitated and shouted out a quick yes. Recently I have given this matter a great deal of thought and have developed what I call "Rinker's Rule of Ten."

Rinker's Rule of Ten is quite simple. When somebody asks me whether something is a collectible, I ask myself one simple question: Would I own ten of them? Think about this for a minute. A real collection requires at least ten items.

Apply this rule to sets of dinner china for twelve, parlor organs, pianos, and sewing machines. No matter how great one of these objects might be to own, what would you do with ten of them? Now it may not seem fair that I selected objects that present storage problems for my example. But in truth, few collectors want to store the bulk of their goodies in boxes. Imagine a collector with four hundred Fraktur birth and baptismal certificates and other illuminated manuscript material associated with the Pennsylvania Germans. When he has utilized all the available wall space in his home hanging his Frakturs, what does he do: hide them in his closet, drawers, basement, attic, or just stop collecting?

I consider my collecting tastes rather universal. More simply put, there are very few things I would not collect given the opportunity, money, and storage space. Recently, however I have seen a number of things, most of which seem to have originated in the decorating shops of large department stores, that have evoked no collecting instinct in me whatsoever. This cannot be a result of my increasing maturity and discriminating taste because, as you have seen, my most recent new collections do not qualify as potential crowd pleasers among the museum-goers.

I have finally forced myself to accept the premise that there are things that will, or perhaps should, never be collected. Some of these objects are purely utilitarian and should be trashed when one is finished with them. Others are decorator items that supply the ticky-tacky tastes of the moment and should be buried when society finally realizes that what was in vogue last year really had a bit of an aroma about it. My list at the moment is not large, but it is growing. It includes washers and dryers, lawnmowers, reproductions of older antique and collectible items, limited-edition collectibles, motel art, stuffed chickens (the latest rage on the flea market circuit), bathroom towels, and magazines such as *National Geographic* or *The Magazine Antiques*. If you ever had to move a twenty-year collection of either of the two magazines, you will understand why they have been included on my list.

Price is a factor of collectibility. It is the collector, not the object itself, that gives value to an object. If a buyer does not exist, there is no value. This is why I stress to individuals trying to understand pricing in the antiques and collectibles field that knowing to whom to sell an object often is worth more than half its actual value.

Just because an object is collected does not mean it has great value. If the number of collectors is small or if the collectors quietly have agreed among themselves to place a limit on what they will pay, the price of an object can remain rather low. False-teeth collectors are an example of the first group; token collectors are an example of the second. I recently joined the Token and Medal Society and began receiving catalogs from a number of individuals who sell tokens through the mail. I was amazed how many tokens were priced below $5. Many were priced between 50¢ and $1. Collectors in this field simply do not seem to be willing to pay high prices. Therefore, prices fluctuate over a very narrow range.

In the collectibles field, the collector comes first, price comes second. We have no "chicken or egg" riddle. Even greater emphasis is placed on "Rinker's Rule of Ten" when one recognizes that the collector comes first. Collectors have to be motivated to collect by the appeal of the collecting category. They have to want to own ten or more objects in a specific category. The category has to attract enough collectors to allow price competition or at least communication among collectors. Not every category of objects can meet these lofty ideals. Fortunately, most do!

I had planned to end here, but in reviewing the manuscript, my associate Ellen Schroy suggested that I swivel around in my chair and make a list of the unusual collectible categories within easy view, just to show my readers that I meant the word "most" in the last sentence of the above paragraph. Have faith, you collectors of things made out of animal parts, faces and banks made from coconuts, laughing toys, tins used to collect money for charities, hats, and modern plastic disks that unlock hotel room doors. You all have company in your chosen collecting fields.

The Excess of Success

THE moose vamoosed. Jessie, the cow, has been jilted.

In one of those quirks of nature, a lovesick moose and a cow captured media headlines and the nation's heart. When the moose wandered into a Shrewsbury, Vermont, pasture in the fall of 1986, he fell in love with Jessie. Although everyone said it couldn't be, the moose stayed for 76 days, ogling, snuggling, and whatever else moose and cows do together, which, according to veterinarians, cannot be much.

Early in January 1987 the moose lost his antlers and apparently his sex drive as well. Bereft of his horns, he left his bovine love and went back into the woods.

But wait, this isn't just an American love story; it's a success story as well. The Carraras, who owned Jessie and the rest of the herd, reacted with traditional entrepreneurial drive. Before long they were selling thousands of "official" moose sweatshirts (short and long sleeve), T-shirts, moose magnets, bumper stickers, records, hats, nightshirts, and four different 5-by-7 pictures of the moose and Jessie.

"The Lonesome Moose," a song, became a hit on the airwaves. Helen and John Kennedy from a nearby hamlet commissioned a special Christmas card that featured Jessie and her suitor. Other "unofficial" moose souvenirs appeared on the market.

Now the moose is gone! Within a few weeks things will return to normal in Shrewsbury. But what about the leftover official and unofficial moose items? What is going to happen to them?

Success breeds excess. Few manufacturers I know are able to accurately predict precisely how many objects will be sold in a holiday season or for a special event. In most cases, they do not run out. They have plenty of unsold goods remaining.

What happened to all the material left over from the recent Bicentennial or Statue of Liberty celebration? How about the remnants from the political campaign trail? Obviously some are remaindered or simply discarded. But I suspect the vast majority is put into storage with the vague hope that someday it can be sold. These are the famous hoards about which collectors and dealers dream. They do exist.

I talked with Lila Carrara about a week after the moose left. She said she was still doing a brisk business in official moose souvenirs. She plans to keep reordering material. I was hoping to detect a note of cautious optimism in her voice, but I did not. I asked if I could call her back in six months to see how sales were at that time. "No problem" was her reply. If I'm right, I think I'll be able to get a good deal on some moose memorabilia.

Speaking of four-legged creatures, can you use 1,600 dozen "Where's the Beef " T-shirts in youth sizes? If so, contact Sam Massimino of Pro Sports, Inc. (R.D. 2, Box 1C, Canonsburg, PA 15317). Pro Sports, Inc., produced more than 100,000 dozen "Where's the Beef " T-shirts for Wendy's.

"The craze died overnight," Sam said. "It took us weeks to admit to ourselves that the end had happened." When production stopped, Pro Sports, Inc., still had more than 3,600 dozen "Where's the Beef " T-shirts.

"We sold all the adult sizes to the flea market dealers for a quarter a T-shirt. The youth sizes, I can't giv'em away, not even for a quarter."

Pro Sports also was lucky enough to be licensed by the Ellis Island Foundation as the authorized headwear manufacturer for the Statue of Liberty celebration. They made fifteen varieties of Statue of Liberty headwear, including the crown hat. Of course, there were the unauthorized versions as well.

Pro Sports still has 160 dozen of the 50,000-dozen regular hats it manufactured. "Of course, I can give you the names of some New York firms whose warehouses are filled with crown hats they'd like to unload," said Sam with a chuckle.

Pro Sports often offers leftover products to local schools and other charitable organizations to be used as fund-raisers. Sometimes they unload the surplus at 25¢ an item just to recover some of their costs.

The most telling remark of all from my interview with Sam, one that should send chills up the spine of the modern craze speculators, is "Once an item is dead, it's dead!"

Recently I talked and corresponded with Joseph A. Blake (P.O. Box 364, Miami Shores, FL 33153), one of the official suppliers to the 1972 Democratic and Republican political conventions in Miami. His specialty was plastic automobile license plates. He produced fourteen styles, some favorable and some unfavorable to each candidate. Among his products are a "McGovern-Eagleton/Unite America" license plate along with its "McGovern-Shriver/Unite America" counterpart.

Unfortunately, his business was not a roaring success. In the three days after Eagleton was replaced by Shriver, he sold 2,700 of the "McGovern-Shriver" plates. But he has close to 200,000 mint-condition plates still in his warehouse. He would like to dispose of the entire lot.

In his letter to me, Blake laments that he has seen 1972 campaign items selling for $10 and more in many areas. At this rate, he has $2 million worth of plastic automobile political license plates in his warehouse. Or does he?

Blake contacted some of the leading dealers in political memorabilia. No luck. He approached some of the leading Americana mail auctions. No luck. He tried the Nixon Library and the Nixon collectors' club. Still no luck. If he advertises and sells the plates individually, I doubt if he will recover the cost of his advertising.

Blake's hoard of plates must be worth something. But even at 10¢ each, it still requires a $20,000 investment to acquire them.

What this illustrates is that hoards are nice, but sometimes they are simply too big to handle. The ideal size of a hoard is from 50 to 250 items. Remember, the number of dedicated collectors in any one category is small. I doubt if the Nixon collectors' club has more than a few hundred members.

None of this solves Blake's problem of his 200,000 license plates. I have sent him a number of suggestions, but none has worked for him. I am out of ideas. Any thoughts for Mr. Blake from my readers?

Developing a "Feel" for Things

THE collectibles field is plagued by reproductions and fakes. How can the collector tell them from the real thing? One of the most overlooked answers is by touching them. In this case, "feel" is a real term, not that famous sixth sense that advanced collectors acquire only after long experience and many mistakes.

The phone company has the right idea. Let your fingers do the walking! Caress every object that you want to buy. Touch it all over; touch every surface. Make love to the object. Connie always tells me that if I touched her like I do my prized collectibles, our marriage would be ten times greater.

Use your fingers to look for wear. Remember, a collectible almost always began life as a utilitarian or play object. As such, it should show some signs of wear. Feel the bottom for rough spots that indicate it had contact with surfaces. Rub the joints to see if they have become separated from use.

Locating wear is not difficult. Pick up the object as though you were going to use it or play with it. Usually, there is only one way to handle the object. Once you have decided how it was held, this is the first place to look for signs of wear. The rubbing of fingers coupled with the natural oils from the skin cause wear and wear marks. Constant use will wear even metals and plastic. Wear marks on pottery and porcelain are a little tougher to spot.

Most collectors are used to using their fingers to examine wooden objects. They know that wood shrinks and warps as it ages. As such, the surface texture should feel wavy, cracks develop where wood is joined with no chances of expansion, and joints become separated. Another key clue in wood is the edges of secondary woods. When the piece is made, those edges are sharp and crisp. Over the years they become rounded as the piece mellows, almost as though they have been smoothed by sandpaper. A good collector knows this feel.

Check the surface texture of the object. A change in the texture generally will indicate a repair or new part. Often when a piece is repaired or refinished, the restorer will not refinish the entire surface. The result is that the repaired area simply feels different from the original surface, which has had years to develop patina or mellow.

Another key to surface texture is the actual feel of the piece. Glass makers changed their formulas for glass over the decades; potteries did the same for glazes. Believe it or not, with enough experience, you can develop a feel for nineteenth-century glass and pottery glazes. For some reason, they simply feel of higher quality. Handle enough earlier pieces and think about this point. You'll join the crowd of experts quickly enough.

Feel for quality of manufacture. When reproductions are made by creating a new mold from an earlier original, detail is lost. The more precise and sharp the decorative elements, the greater the chance that you are handling an original.

Another key is consistency in manufacture. Remember, this was the norm historically, not the exception. The piece simply has to feel the same everywhere. Quality tends to be consistent throughout original objects.

Feel the weight of the object. You'll be surprised when you put an original object in one hand and a reproduction in the other how frequently the reproduction weighs more than the original. One of the reasons for this is that reproductions tend to be made of thicker material, whether porcelain or glass. The thicker material allows for greater tolerance in manufacturing. Remember that the reproduction manufacturer is looking for speed and quantity, not quality.

The more original objects you handle, the less you will be fooled by the reproductions. Satin glass is a good example. The next time you are at an antiques show and see some satin glass, ask the dealer if you can handle it. The feel of old satin glass is unique. The modern reproductions simply are unable to capture it.

One of the reasons why I accept so many invitations to visit private collectors is to view and handle their collections. As I touch and caress each piece, I create and capture a mental image of how it feels in my hand. I'll use this later in the field to check the pieces I see.

Don't know any collectors? Don't worry. The best collections to study, where you can handle all the objects you wish, are auction previews. Few or no questions asked. A fun day in New York is a preview of a Christie's or Sotheby's sale, where you can touch the material being auctioned to your heart's content. However, you can do the same thing at regional auction houses, as well as during the morning hours before a country sale.

Now get out there and have some fun touching things.

Fakes, Reproductions, and Copycats

EVERY collector must be constantly alert for fakes and reproductions within his or her collecting category. However, many collectors mistakenly assume that an object is reproduced, faked, or copied only after it has become classified as an antique or collectible. The truth is quite the opposite. Reproductions, fakes, knockoffs, call them what you will, follow immediately after an object is successfully marketed.

The Cabbage Patch doll is an excellent example. Counterfeit Cabbage Patch dolls were available within six months of the mass-marketing of the original Cabbage Patch doll. In many cases, for example, T-shirts, copies can be on the market in a matter of days or weeks. A subtle change in design, lettering, slogan, or spelling of a name is all that is needed.

When counterfeit material first appears in the market, the manufacturer of the original product goes to great length to inform the public about the forgery and how to distinguish it from the original. In addition, the manufacturer takes legal steps to stop the sale of the counterfeit items.

However, information about counterfeit and reproduction items is frequently lost or forgotten once the product is no longer popular or has been withdrawn from the market. Several months ago, a reader wrote to me inquiring about a Southern Comfort belt buckle he had acquired at a flea market. The owner had the item in his possession for over ten years. Fortunately, I remembered the furor caused in the early 1970s by a rash of fake belt buckles, among which were the Southern Comfort and Wells Fargo buckles. At the time, there were several articles written in the trade papers about these totally new fabrications. When I tried to find information on them in 1987, I could not. The opportunity to fool a young collector is greater now than at the time when the buckles were issued.

What about the counterfeit and reproduction items made during the 1920s and 1930s? Just like the originals they mimicked, they now have the signs of age and antiquity that collectors all too frequently rely upon to tell an original from a modern fake. The sources that documented these early counterfeits and reproductions are few. It is almost impossible to find copies of them.

Recently I had an opportunity to read Ruth Webb Lee's *Antique Fakes and Reproductions*, 7th edition (Wellesley Hills, MA: Lee Publications, 1950), a book that chronicles the early American glass and pattern-glass reproductions of the 1920 to 1950 period. These reproductions fool many current dealers and collectors. Recently the Charles E. Tuttle Company reprinted all of Ruth Webb Lee's books except *Antique Fakes and Reproductions*. This oversight is a tragedy.

Dorothy Hammond deserves praise for her two pioneering books, *Confusing Collectibles: A Guide to the Identification of Contemporary Objects* (Wallace-Homestead, 1969) and *More Confusing Collectibles: A Guide to the Identification of Reproductions* (privately printed, 1972). These books are an excellent source for the reproductions that were produced in the 1950s and 1960s. Unfortunately, neither is available.

One of the more amusing ironies in this story is that collecting counterfeit and fake objects has become an obsession with some collectors. The pattern-glass reproductions of the 1920s and 1930s are now valued about the same as the originals. Most Disney collections contain several unlicensed Disney items; the same is true of my Hopalong Cassidy collection.

Lawrence L. Wonsch's *Hummel Copycats with Values: A Guide to Those Other Hummels* (Wallace-Homestead, 1987) is a new publication that should be on every collector's shelf. Wonsch has provided an excellent case study of the counterfeit and reproduction question. The general conclusions that can be drawn from his work apply to all collecting categories, not just to Hummel figurines.

First, Wonsch indicates that the source for counterfeits is not limited to one country or geographic area. Hummel imitators were found in England, Germany, Hong Kong, Japan, Spain, and even the United States. Second, he clearly documents that the imitators arrived on the scene simultaneously with the issuing of Hummel figurines by Goebel. Design variations are there, but they are subtle. During World War II, when Goebel's Hummel figurines were in short supply, Herbert Dubler, Inc., of New York, trading as The House of Ars Sacra, and Beswick in England made and copyrighted figurines based on the actual designs of Berta Hummel.

Third, it is a common assumption by collectors that counterfeit and reproduction copies do not match the quality of the original product. This is not always true. Wonsch demonstrates clearly that many of the Hummel copycats actually met or came extremely close to Goebel-quality figurines. Fourth, Wonsch deserves credit for providing a wealth of photographic detail to show the subtle changes in design in many of the copycat pieces. In many cases, Wonsch identifies three to four variations of a single Goebel Hummel figurine. The change may be limited only to the shape of the base or the color of a hat.

Finally, Wonsch documents the Hummel-copycat spinoffs, a method used by many manufacturers to capitalize on the popularity of a collecting craze. Hummel figurines were made in glass and metal instead of the customary porcelain. Hummel-inspired figurines appeared on cards, bookends, salt and pepper shakers, ashtrays, lamps, planters, wall vases, revolving musical boxes, and many more objects, none of which were made by Goebel. Designers developed figurines that were inspired by but never found among Berta Hummel's drawings.

Fakes, reproductions, and copycats are an aspect of collecting with which all collectors must deal. Their presence should never discourage collecting. Initially, collectors need to follow one simple rule: "Collect what you know." As you learn to identify the fakes, reproductions, and copycats in your collecting field, you will probably add some of them to your collection of originals. In a way, the fakes, reproductions, and copycats are needed to tell the total story.

[illegible] exterior [illegible] [illegible] and [illegible] [illegible] the [illegible] The [illegible] [illegible] World [illegible] that many of [illegible] [illegible] [illegible] [illegible] [illegible]

Finally, Wiener commented, [illegible] [illegible] [illegible] [illegible] [illegible] and [illegible] [illegible] [illegible] [illegible] these used figures were made in glass and metal instead of the customary porce-[illegible] [illegible] [illegible] lamps, planters, wall vases, [illegible] [illegible] [illegible] [illegible]

[illegible] [illegible] [illegible] [illegible] [illegible] in a way the [illegible] [illegible] producers and copywriters, in order to sell the [illegible].

Part 3
What You Need to Know About Pricing

What's a Fair Price?

A reader wrote: "Would you know where we could take a stack of very old *Life* and *Look* magazines, postcards, and very old comic books to get the best prices? We have talked with some comic book collectors, but they do not offer near book value for these fine comics."

The frustrations of this reader are experienced by almost all private individuals who want to sell their collectibles but have little or no understanding of how the collectibles marketplace works or the fact that collectibles have many potential values depending on the buyer. I hope the following will help my reader find a buyer and a fair price at which to sell; but I suspect it is not the information my reader wants to hear.

Using price guides is fraught with dangers. They make people greedy. Novices turn to them for guidance without knowing how to evaluate the prices. They locate their collectibles or something similar to what they own and think that the listed prices are what they should receive when selling their objects.

The introduction to *Warman's Americana & Collectibles,* third edition (Warman Publishing Company, 1988) contains a section headlined "Buyer's Guide, Not Seller's Guide." Unfortunately, most users do not read it, or choose to ignore it if they do. It states: "*Warman's Americana & Collectibles* is designed to be a buyer's guide, a guide to what you would have to pay to purchase an object on the open market from a dealer or collector. *It is not a seller's guide to prices*. People frequently make this mistake and are deceiving themselves by doing so."

Price guides should be viewed in the same context as a retail catalog from a department store. Admittedly, the prices are not as fixed and the exact items are not actually for sale. However, any seller must understand that the prices in a price guide represent what a *serious* collector will pay. As such, they reflect the highest potential value for an object to a very select, very small group of people.

An Elvis Presley guitar in its original box has a book value of $400 to $600. But it has that value only to an Elvis Presley collector and only to an Elvis collector who does not already own one. Someone who collects Avon bottles might not be willing to pay $10 for the Elvis guitar.

How do you find the serious collectors who are willing to pay the top dollar? The answer is simple — with a great deal of hard work that involves both time and money.

The biggest component of any collectible's value is the buyer. Without the buyer, the collectible is worth very little. Knowing to whom to sell a collectible is worth between fifty and sixty-five percent of its value. It is not fair to assume that you are going to find a "top buyer" walking along the street. Dealers and others have spent years learning who the "top buyers" are in each specialized collectible category. Furthermore, they keep this information secret, just as most collectors keep their sources for buying collectibles a secret.

Few owners and novices are willing to invest their time to study the market or spend their money for research material, membership in collectors' clubs, attendance at educational seminars, and advertising in trade papers, all of which are necessary to reach the serious collectors. They want a quick sale at the highest price without any of the work. They turn to a dealer in hopes of achieving this end, expecting the dealer to pay them the same price as a serious collector. Wrong, very wrong!

Again, I direct your attention to the third edition of *Warman's Americana & Collectibles*: "If you have an object in this book and wish to sell it, you should expect to receive approximately 35 to 40% of the value listed. If the object cannot be resold quickly, expect to receive even less." A collectible may be sold and resold several times before it is bought by a collector. Each person who handles the object along the way made a profit. In fact, the majority of the final selling price of any collectible contains a large profit factor. The intrinsic value is often quite small.

Dealers have a right to make a profit and deserve the profit that they make. The expenses are considerable for a dealer with an open shop or who works the show circuit regularly. Overhead must be paid before they can pay themselves a salary. Selling collectibles is one of the hardest ways of making a living.

Selling collectibles is labor- and capital-intensive. When a dealer buys a collection it must be sorted, prepared for sale, researched, stored, displayed, and merchandised. This takes time, and time is money.

Paper ephemera and collectibles such as comics, magazines, newspapers, and postcards, are especially labor-intensive. While some material may sell quickly, the greater bulk will remain in inventory from six months to five years. Visit a comic book shop. Look at the amount of inventory. The dealer does not own this material on credit; he has to buy it. He cannot afford to pay top dollar. He should not be expected to pay it.

Furthermore, the ability to grade the precise condition and scarcity of any collectible requires years of study and experience. You don't learn this from reading books. You learn by handling objects and immersing yourself in the marketplace. Collectors want to believe that the material that they own is rare and in the best condition. Ninety-nine point nine percent of the time they are wrong. It usually is several condition grades below their own estimate.

It is almost impossible for amateur collectors to judge their own collectibles objectively. If their objects hold childhood or personal memories it is totally impossible. As an appraiser, I spend a great deal of my time telling people their treasures are not "gold" at all, but items readily available in the marketplace. Hundreds or thousands of examples may exist. If you are not in the right place, you do not see them.

It is time to answer the question: "Where can I get the best price?" If, after reading and thinking about the above, my reader continues to believe that he can achieve book prices, the answer is simple: "Nowhere." A good price is a price at which both the buyer and seller are happy. If my reader will not be happy with anything less than top dollar, he had better accept the possibility that he is going to die owning his collectibles.

You must determine the market level at which you are planning to sell. If you are willing to invest the time and money to find the serious collector, the top buyer, then do it. However, ask yourself if the potential profit justifies the effort.

If you sell to a dealer, set your price accordingly. Remember, you should not expect to get more than fifty percent of the prices in a *current* price guide. Since these prices are based on collectibles in very good condition, any condition grade below this should lower your expectations.

Finally, after you do sell your collectibles, walk away. Forget it. Don't get upset if a dealer doubles, triples, or quadruples his money on some or all of the collectibles that you sold him. First, be happy you made some money. Second, remember that the dealer's hard work and experience has provided him with the one valuable piece of information that you did not have: the name of the collector who would pay top price. Be happy for him too.

Price Guides: A Curse or a Blessing?

SOMEONE recently asked me, "What do you think of price guides?" "They are a curse," I exclaimed. "But you edit price guides." "Alas, all too true," I sighed.

Within the past fifteen years, the antiques and collectibles field has been inundated with general and specific price guides on almost every conceivable collecting category. Did you know there are three price guides to lightning-rod balls? Do you care?

The avalanche of price guides has had a profound effect on the field. It has increased the level of greed manyfold. Once an object has been purchased, no one wants to sell it until they have located it in a price guide and found out what it is "really worth." It doesn't make any difference what they paid for it; they want the most they can get for it.

Individuals rarely question the prices that they find in the price guides. How do they know the prices are right? It is time to ask two major questions about the authors and editors of any price guide: What is their expertise and sources, and what are the motives behind their writing the price guide?

Collectors frequently accept an author's or editor's expertise without question. This is a major mistake. The antiques and collectibles field has become a source of instant experts. People think they are experts the minute they own fifty objects in a collecting category, inform you they are writing a book about a category, or help organize a collectors' club. All too often it is the blind leading the blind.

One result of this instant expertise is the proliferation of priced picture guides. One good example is Linda Baker's *Modern Toys: American Toys, 1930-1980*, containing illustrations of toys produced by more than seventy-five toy manufacturers between 1930 and 1980.

Note what I said — illustrations. It's time to rephrase that famous question of "Where's the beef?" to "Where's the research?" Historical background is presented for only a select few of the toy manufacturers. Why waste time and book space with this information? But not only does the book lack information about the manufacturers, it provides only a partial listing at best of the products of these manufacturers. I happen to have some interest in the All-Fair Toy Company, primarily because of my game collection. Baker's book does not even contain actual examples, just a copy of an ad from a 1930 *Child Life* magazine. Big help!

While it is unfair to expect a price guide to contain a listing of every product that a company produces, it is fair to expect that the listing will be detailed enough to give an idea of the range of material produced by that company. I know that the All-Fair Toy Company made far more than the half-dozen toys pictured in it's 1930s ad.

Furthermore, a price guide whose title promises comprehensiveness has an obligation to provide it or a reasonable explanation as to why it is not provided. It would not be difficult to prepare a list containing several hundred companies that made toys between 1930 and 1980 that are not found in Baker's book. Two giants that immediately come to mind are Sun Rubber and Duncan, the yo-yo king.

Baker's book seems like a glorification of her own personal collection. Her introduction reads: "Most of the toys pictured here are from my own collection. If a toy belongs to someone else or the photograph was taken by someone else, credit is given beneath the photo." Only 77 of the 737 illustrations were credited to someone else, just slightly above ten percent.

I think that any price guide that provides a majority of the illustrations from the author's or editor's personal collection must be questioned both in terms of comprehensiveness and accuracy. It is an all too common practice for someone to prepare a price guide featuring the material from their collection and then sell the collection at the prices listed in the book, and often even slightly more. Individuals buy because they rely on the authority of the price guide. It is not difficult to disguise the source of the material being offered for sale.

Another practice of some authors and editors has been to price those items in their guides that they wish to sell high and those items that they wish to buy low. This practice is difficult to spot unless one deals actively in that collecting category. But the practice is prevalent and talked about openly in the field.

If I have been successful thus far, I have convinced you to start questioning the qualifications and motives of the individuals who have authored or edited the price guides. Now it is time to get you to question the prices themselves.

The prices found in price guides are not absolutes—so firm that to deviate from them represents a sin of major proportion. If done well, the books are at best guides to what the author or editor thinks the pieces will bring in an average market situation. Note the emphasis on "think." Few authors or editors actually witness the sale of the objects they price. Those who double as collectors and have purchased the objects are not going to tell you what they really paid for them, especially if they were bought at bargain prices. They will list what they think the object is worth; or, perhaps more correctly phrased, what they *wish* the object was worth now that they own it.

Further, the prices in a price guide usually are based upon what a collector from that category will pay for the object. It assumes an interest on the part of the buyer. The result is that the prices represent a "high end" pricing structure. Unless the seller can locate one of these collectors, the prices are not valid.

Does this mean that all antiques and collectibles price guides are bad? Absolutely not! Many price guides are excellent and contain a wealth of research information, comprehensive listings, and accurate pricing. When you find one, you will have no trouble recognizing it. You can use my two Warman guides and Kovel's, Shroeder's, and *The Antique Trader Weekly's* guides as models in the general category. Ted Hake's button guides are excellent examples in that specific category.

Learn to use price guides for what they are—guides. This is a lesson you should never forget.

Magic Numbers

THE next time you visit an antiques shop or stop by a booth at a flea market or show, look closely at the price tags. Carefully analyze the prices. In all probability, you will be struck by a rather startling observation. Certain prices will seem to repeat themselves over and over again. Apparently the dealer believes that certain numbers have sale magic.

These magic numbers are almost universal in the trade. On objects that would normally sell below $100, the key numbers are $85, $65, $45, $20, $12, and $8. Each number can be rationalized. For example, $45 is close to $50, but it seems much more reasonable to the buyer. Simply repeat the process for the other numbers.

The inherent assumptions involving magic sale numbers are worth considering. First, they create pricing plateaus. The dealer fits every object neatly into one of these plateaus, thus simplifying his pricing efforts. A dealer relying on magic sale numbers is susceptible to the temptation to force an object into a higher profit bracket. By accepting the process of price simplification, the dealer has lost the ability to see the subtleties in his merchandise.

Second, the magic sale numbers indicate that the dealer divorces what he pays for an object from the sale price of the object. I believe strongly in the dealer's right to double or triple his money on any purchase he makes. A dealer, whether doing shows or managing a shop, has a high overhead and a great deal of money invested in inventory. If dealers double or triple their return on every object they purchase, their price tags would reflect a wide range of prices. But in reality, dealers tend not to do this.

Most want top dollar for their merchandise. A bargain purchase by a dealer simply means the opportunity to turn a great profit. It is the rare dealer that passes along the bargain price to his customers.

Too many young dealers want to start at the top and skip the apprenticeship that is essential in creating a great dealer. Historically, dealers served an extended apprenticeship. They earned and worked their way to the top slowly, learning as they went. As they moved up the ladder, the quality of their merchandise and the prices they achieved increased. Along the way, dealers were content with modest profits at the lower and middle levels, preferring to turn merchandise rather than make the ultimate killing. In the 1980s the traditional pattern broke down. In my opinion, it is a change for the worse. The field would benefit greatly from a return to a tiered level of dealing, where dealers on each level were satisfied with the profits they made and the position they enjoyed.

A second set of magic numbers occurs at auctions. Have you ever been at an auction where two individuals hotly contest a piece that finally was sold for $100 or $500? Why did the bidder at $90 or $95 refuse to go to $105 or $110? In terms of actual dollars, the difference is slight. In psychological terms, however, the difference is enormous.

I know. I recently attended an auction where I had asked the auctioneer to put up something for sale so that I could leave. As the object was being sold, I made the mistake of getting in on the bids ending in five—$65, $75, etc. When I bid $95 and my opponent bid $100, I quit. I had the money to go higher; I wanted the object. But I simply could not do it.

For whatever reason, certain numbers stop the bidding. Over the years, the lowest number keeps getting higher and higher. Today few bidders feel threatened by $25 or $50. Given the number of items that I saw exceeding $100 at the auction I attended, I suspect that this number is no longer much of a barrier either.

A third magic number, the "throw-away" money number, is of major concern to anyone buying or selling collectibles. It is the amount of money that any buyer is willing to spend recklessly on an object.

During the 1987 Antiques and Collectibles Information Service seminar at Lehigh University, I had the opportunity to explore this concept in detail with Susanne Smokoska of Saginaw, Michigan. Susanne contends, and I agree, that there is an amount of money that individuals have in their wallets when they visit a show or flea market that they are planning to spend, no matter what. In the late 1970s, this amount fluctuated between $10 and $15. Susanne feels that the amount has now risen to $20 or $25. Actually, I think the amount is closer to $35.

If our assumption is correct, a wise dealer can increase his sales by offering a number of objects in very good condition that are priced below $30. The more pizzazz the object has, the more likely it is to sell. It is just this type of selling that has the potential to create many new collectors.

The "throw-away" money number is an important barometer in determining how a dealer views his or her position in the market. I have been in booths and shops where it almost is impossible to find an object priced below $100. This dealer is not out to create new collectors; he prefers to work only within the established portion of the market. In my opinion, the wisest dealer has something in his inventory to fit everyone's pocketbook.

Keep these numbers in mind the next time you visit a flea market, shop, or show. But do not let them dominate your thinking. Remember, the real fun in collecting collectibles is the sheer joy of it. Collectibles allow you to recapture your childhood under the guise of preserving material from the past. Be a kid again. Live a little.

Maxwell's Ultimate Unit Theory

MEETING Jimmy Maxwell is an immediate adrenalin injection. Within the first minute of any conversation, he says something that sets my mind to thinking so hard I cannot turn it off for days. During a recent conversation Jim told me about his Ultimate Unit Theory. I asked him if he would mind if I shared it with you.

"Go ahead," was his reply. "I just wonder how many will take it seriously."

Scientists have long held that the ultimate formula that will explain how our universe functions will be simple and beautiful in form. The more I study the collectibles field, the more I am convinced that it can be quantified into a series of simply understood, obvious, and beautiful theories of operation. Maxwell's Ultimate Unit Theory fits this pattern.

The ultimate unit is that object, the one in ten thousand or a million, in any collectibles category that will be the most sought-after object by the richest collector prepared to pay the highest price. We are talking about THE piece to own—the piece that is most talked about, rarely photographed, and seen only by the most select of the collector fraternity. We are talking about a legend.

Don't tell me that such pieces do not exist. You have all heard about the rumors of a mechanical bank worth in excess of $250,000 or of a piece of Tupperware that sold for over $1000. The ultimate collectible unit is not sold in the auction sector but in the realm of private dealings.

Maxwell's Ultimate Unit Theory contends that the price of the ultimate unit continues to rise no matter what the present status of the category as a whole is doing. The category could be stable, running, or declining in value. It doesn't matter. The ultimate unit keeps going up.

The treadle sewing machine market is a good example. Most common machines were made in the millions. An average treadle machine brings between $50 and $100. Is it then safe to conclude that the ultimate unit might command $500 to $1,000? Absolutely not. I recently talked with a collector who paid in excess of $6,000 for a treadle sewing machine. I suspect the price for the ultimate unit is probably higher.

Rarity and condition are the two keys to identifying the ultimate unit. First, there must be only one or two examples known. Ideally, they should be in private collections. Second, the piece must be as close as possible to "mint-in-the-box." The word "original" has an almost reverential meaning when describing the ultimate unit.

I asked Jim if he had any predictions about which collectibles category might see a spectacular rise in the value of the ultimate units in the next decade. His answer nearly knocked me for a loop. Jim predicts that the market will see the first $100,000 teddy bear by the year 2000.

In my opinion the teddy bear market is dead. By "dead" I mean that the price for most bears is stable, not rising or falling more than plus or minus five percent during a year. The teddy bear market is oversaturated with material, is not developing new collectors, has more books on the subject than anyone has the time or desire to read, and has reached a price level where most collectors say enough is enough.

It is true that record prices are being set at auction for a few units at the top. The $5,000 teddy bear has been replaced by the $8,000-plus teddy bear. However, many of these are being paid by dealers. Is it their last gasp trying to prop up a fading market, or do they honestly expect to turn a handsome profit on their purchases? My bet is the former.

Now comes the beauty of Maxwell's Ultimate Unit Theory. It works best in a dead—stable—market. As the teddy bear market enters a period of price stability, the legend of the ultimate unit spreads. Rumors spread that one teddy bear has brought a price far in excess of any record at auction.

Enter the ultimate collector, the person who must have what no one else can own. Price is no object; he never intends to resell the piece. The collector's appetite grows as the legend increases. Finally, the piece surfaces, he buys it, and his wants are filled for the moment. The quest has been completed. The legend lives.

Some dealers specialize in finding the ultimate units and their collectors. Jim Maxwell is one for the fields he covers. He assures me that he is nowhere near as totally dedicated to the pursuit as he was ten years ago. But you should have seen his eyes light up when he talked about the $100,000 teddy bear.

I was going to bet him a dinner that it would not happen by the duomillenium. Then I thought carefully about it. All he needs is the incentive to do it.

I am responsible for enough madness in the collectible field already. I certainly don't need to add this to my list.

The Whole Is Equal to the Sum of the Parts

I am angry. If I wait until I calm down and temper my remarks, the impact of what I am about to say will be lessened. I do not want that to happen.

During a visit to a local antiques and collectibles mall, I was drawn to a booth devoted almost exclusively to cowboy collectibles, one of my favorite interests. I spotted a blue Hopalong Cassidy lunch box priced at $32 on one of the top shelves in the booth. When I examined the lunch box, I noticed the thermos was missing. Almost immediately I saw it on the shelf below. Its price tag read $24. What the (#* + ?%?*#!) is going on? I thought to myself.

A quick glance produced an all-too-obvious answer. Other collectibles in the booth suffered the same fate. The dealer was disassembling complete units and pricing the individual parts separately. There is only one motivation for such action: GREED. I make a big distinction between greed and an honest profit.

A special place in hell should be reserved for the despicable collectors and dealers who purposely disassemble complete collectibles. This is the collectible equivalent of rape. In my opinion these individuals deserve our strongest condemnation and contempt. They should be shunned.

The galling habit of disassembling complete units has long been an established practice among print dealers and decorators. They tear apart atlases into individual sheets and remove engraved and decorated plates from books, mat and frame the individual items, and reap a far greater reward than from the sale of the atlas or book alone. Think of the thousands of single sheets from medieval manuscripts that flood the market. In most cases, the value of the frame exceeds the value of the object in it.

I am not naive. It is not realistic to believe that every collectible unit will be found intact. Objects are played with and used; parts get lost or broken. I have a son, a daughter, and a granddaughter. I know.

Should the dealer or collector discard or ignore a collectible because it is not complete? Certainly not. Parts have value. But disassembled parts should not be *over*valued. The true value of any part is the percentage of the cost of the whole that it represents. Any value paid over that percentage is lost when and if the complete unit is reassembled. This is the ideal; it is not how the market works.

In the collectibles field the sum of the parts often far exceeds the value of the whole. Price depends on what someone is willing to pay. If collectors are willing to pay higher prices for the parts than the whole, then the market responds accordingly.

This approach has important ramifications for the collector who assembles a large collection and then wants a premium price for the collection as a whole when he or she sells it. If the sum of the parts is greater than the whole, the buyer should expect to pay less, not more, for the collection as a whole. Why do you think so many collections are sold at auction? The seller realizes that maximum return is based on the objects sold individually.

There is only one collectible area—objects that will be used primarily for utilitarian purposes, such as china dinner services—where I think charging a premium price is justified. Replacement services have to maintain large inventories. Rarely do their customers want a full set of china, glass, or silver; they want one or two examples to replace something that was broken. When a replacement service breaks a full set, it needs to recover its initial investment in the sale of a relatively few pieces. This is not an unfair approach.

But a Hopalong Cassidy lunch box is not a utilitarian object. No collector is going to pack one full of peanut butter and jelly sandwiches and take it to work. The lunch box is going to serve as a decorative object, part of a collection to be displayed and viewed. The distinction is subtle between a vintage object that still has utilitarian value and one whose value is purely decorative. But it is worth making.

Is it possible to put a stop to the practice of valuing the parts at a greater value than the whole? The answer is no. The fault does not rest with dealers alone. Collectors have to share part of the blame. The dealers would stop the practice if the collectors would either refuse to buy a collectible that is not complete or pay a premium price for a part. But collectors themselves are out of control. Their desire to own frequently overwhelms their common sense.

Purists argue that they are buying the part in hopes of finding the rest of the parts and putting the unit back together. I would accept this argument except that most collectors are willing to pay the premium price rather demanding a reduced cost.

Some collectors contend that they did not know the item was part of a larger unit. What's the matter? Are they too lazy to do research? I continue to be amazed at how little collectors know about their collecting field. Be suspicious. A bowlegged plastic cowboy that cannot stand on his own two feet has to fit onto something. If he is not wearing a hat or his guns, something is missing. Must a collector be hit on the head with a hammer?

The group of collectors that earns my wrath more than the others are those individuals who break up complete sets after they purchase them. An excellent example are game board collectors. All they want are the boards. They frequently throw out the rest of the game. Dumb, dumb, dumb.

I have vented my anger. I would like to end on a positive note. The individuals that I have talked about here represent a small fraction of the collectors and dealers in our field. At the same antiques and collectible mall where I saw the disassembled Hopalong Cassidy lunch box, I also found a complete unit priced at $38 at another dealer's booth. Someone cares; and I think this is far more typical than the despicable cases.

Adding Value: The Original Box

IN the storage space above the closet in the entrance hall at Schtee Fens, my home, are two boxes filled with empty boxes. They remain as a monument to that gene which determines who is a "saver" and who is not—the one that my son, currently in the army, inherited from me.

Harry Jr. must have heard me complain once too often about those stupid individuals who never saved the boxes in which things came. He determined early in his youth not to make the same mistake. As a result, he owns a significant collection of empty boxes. If hard pressed, I doubt if he could locate among his possessions the original contents of over half the boxes. Why not simply throw out those boxes?

Stop and think for a moment. How many Mickey Mouse watches have you seen for sale? Now, how many Mickey Mouse watch boxes have you seen? Is it possible the original box may be worth more than the original watch? In this and many other cases, the answer may be yes.

Many collectibles originally had boxes or packaging that in essence was part of the total presentation of the piece. It is a reality that almost the entire game collecting craze centers on the lithographic image on the box cover more than it does on the contents of the games. A collector will accept a few missing game pieces; he will not accept damage to the box cover.

If a collectible had a box that contained any type of advertising relating to that collectible, then the highest value for that collectible is tied to its being in its original box. Collectors use the term "MIB," meaning "mint-in-the-box." They don't mean just the product. They also mean the box.

What does this mean in respect to pricing collectibles. If the original box or packing was elaborate, it adds between twenty to forty percent to the price of the collectible. If the box is average, i.e., it has some advertising and printing beyond a listing of the product name, it adds ten to twenty percent to the price of the collectible.

Likewise, the box itself can become an independent collectible, especially if it was associated with a famous cartoon, movie, radio, or television personality. I am reluctant to make this point because I can envision some dealers separating a collectible from its original box and pricing the two items separately to get the maximum price. Such greed mongers deserve the most heinous of demises.

Well, now back to my son's empty box collection. Those empty boxes all relate to *Star Wars* and other crazes from the early 1970s. Think of all those kids who built the models, played with the toys and figures, and wore the watches. When they turn thirty-five and become enamored with the nostalgia craze of their youth, they'll find the models (put together with varying degrees of skills), the figures and toys, and even the watches. But will they find the boxes?

Honestly, if he holds them long enough, I think Harry Jr. has the makings of a small fortune in that space above the entrance hall closet. Now, let's see. If he is going to make that kind of money in the future, maybe I ought to charge him rent. Or, better yet, maybe I'll charge him a box or two a year and add them to my own collection of empty boxes. I'm no dummy.

The Value of Number One

A local bank's television commercial touts the fact that "you're Number One." Throughout America we vie with each other to document or inventively create "firsts" for our communities. Does anyone really care that the first oatmeal in America was ground at a mill in Bethlehem, Pennsylvania? What is this fascination that we have of wanting to own the first one of something?

In many aspects of the collectibles field, there are people who specialize in collecting only the first issue in a series. Among the categories where this madness prevails are baseball and other bubble gum cards, books (first editions), comic books, dolls, limited-edition collector plates, magazines, newspapers, and postcards.

I almost dread the annual arrival of Robert M. Overstreet's *The Comic Book Price Guide*, distributed by Harmony Books of New York. I am staggered by the prices he quotes for some of the number-one issues.

The 1986–87 edition lists a near-mint-condition Marvel Comics No. 1 (introduced "Sub-mariner and Human Torch") at $23,000, Action Comics No. 1 (introduced "Superman") at $18,500, "Superman" No. 1 at $17,500, Whiz Comics No. 1 at $13,000, and "Batman" No. 1 at $6,500.

These are only suggested prices. In a way, they do not totally reflect reality. I talked with Don Thompson of *Comics Buyer's Guide*, a weekly newspaper published by Krause Publications (700 East State Street, Iola, WI 54990). Don reports a Marvel Comics No. 1 has sold for a record $36,500 and an Action Comics No. 1 at $40,000. These are documented sales. Don believes higher prices have been realized on the private market and simply not reported.

Overstreet even reports that an avid collector traded his house for a stack of seventy to eighty comics from the "Mile High" collection, a special collection assembled by Edgar Church, who purchased and carefully stored one copy of every comic book published from the late 1930s through the mid-1950s. The comics constituted the equity, with the remaining mortgage payments being taken over by the new house owner. To say the banker handling he transaction "was beside himself" appears to me to be a mild understatement.

If the first issues are worth vast sums of money, what is the second issue worth? Overstreet lists a mint Marvel Mystery Comics No. 2 (the continuation of Marvel Comics No. 1) at $4,085, Action Comics No. 2 at $4,200, "Superman" No. 2 at $1,925, Whiz No. 2 at $2,200, and "Batman" No. 2 at $1,925. In no case is the figure for the second issue higher than 30% of the value of the first issue, and in most cases it's less.

What is true for comic books is true for the field as a whole. In general the second item in an older series sells among collectors for approximately ten to thirty percent of the value of the first item in the series. Lower series numbers sell for even less.

Have you ever thought about how much sense this approach of valuing "firsts" so highly really makes? The second item in a series is frequently designed by the same individual, manufactured in equal quality to the first, and often distributed at the same time or shortly thereafter. In a series of limited-edition collector items, selecting the object that comes first is a completely arbitrary decision made by an employee at the manufacturing plant.

Collecting based solely on the "first" criteria does not take into consideration aesthetics, quality, or pizzazz. Try looking at a full series of collector dolls purely from a design point of view. Maybe the second or the eighth doll in the series appeals to you more. But, which one generally has the greatest value? Why, it's the first one, of course.

A great deal of the "first" market is based on rarity. Collectors tend to equate "first" with rarest or hardest to find. Two attitudes foster this myth. First, collectors assume that only a few of the first item were made because the manufacturer was testing the market. Second, collectors feel that the first item has been around long enough for most of them to have been thrown away.

Like it or not, collectibles were mass-produced. Never loose sight of this. Nothing scares out more examples than a newspaper account or trade rumor of a record price for a number-one object. The speculators in Action Comics No. 1 or Marvel Comics No. 1 live with the fear that someone may find a stash of fifty mint-condition comics in a box in an old warehouse somewhere. If this would happen, the value of their comics would plummet overnight.

"First" collectors have a companion in crime — the "oldest" collector. When collectors cannot have the "first" of something, they try to have the oldest. Bethlehem cannot boast about having the first fire engine made in America, but it can about having the oldest. It seems the thrifty Moravians bought a used fire engine from London and brought it to America. It is older than the first fire engine made in this country.

How often have you visited a collector and heard him or her brag, "This is the oldest example known?" So what? Few craftspeople or manufacturers make their best example on their first attempt. In fact, you would expect them to make better and better things over time.

Yet, it is the oldest thing that frequently is the highest-priced item in the collectibles field. The 1895 Bing and Grondahl Christmas plate lists at $4,000; the 1896 plate at $2,000. Looking at them merely from a design point of view and not being told which one is the oldest, I suspect a fair number of individuals would choose the second.

The Hummel collectors, with the price they are willing to pay for a figure based on the year it was made, determined by the mark, are another example of the craziness of this oldest philosophy. The Barnyard Hero, figure 195/2/0, is valued at $320 with the crown mark and $185 with the full bee mark.

Think for a moment. The figure probably was made in the same mold. Hummel did not change molds each time the firm changed marks. Each figure was hand painted. Suppose the person who painted the crown mark figure was an apprentice painter and the person who painted the full bee figure was the best person in the factory. The aesthetic level of the second figure would be much higher than the first figure.

Make a difference? No, it does not. Somehow collectors have gotten their values distorted.

I think a lot of the value found in number-one items and the oldest item is largely speculative. As long as enough other collectors are willing to fuel the market, the values hold.

But sometimes the bubble bursts. Remember when the 1971 Hummel Christmas plate was selling above $3,000? Well, today you easily can find one between $600 and $800. How long will the comic book mania last? I suspect that we may be reaching a peak.

The smart collector evaluates all aspects of a collectible before making a purchase. While something being number one or the oldest is important, it must be put into perspective with other pricing considerations. If you don't and get burned, don't worry. You are not the first.

The Collectible as an *Objet d'Art*

ONE of the principal problems with antiques is that far too many of them are in museums, where a sanctimonious group of individuals, known as curators, conducts esoteric research about them and exercises a guardianship that ideally allows only the "privileged and deserving" an opportunity to view their prized possessions. Antiques are treated as hallowed treasures, placed on pedestals, stands, or walls to be worshiped and admired from afar. When was the last time you heard anyone laugh in a museum?

Thus far, the twentieth-century collectible has escaped this mantle of deification. A recent Diet Coke commercial stated the best approach to take toward collectibles: "Just for the Fun of It." Face it, collectibles are fun. They are neat. You do not need a cloak of respectability to justify saving and collecting them.

The good times may be ending. There are signs of danger on the horizon. Sotheby's super-hype surrounding the sale of the Andy Warhol collection has everyone collectible crazy. Museums have discovered twentieth-century collectibles. Museum exhibits on electrical appliances and cowboy collectibles have already been held.

Leading the attack on the fun aspect of collectibles is a group of dealers and collectors who view the twentieth-century collectible primarily as a big-ticket item. The key to their success is converting the collectible from a fun-filled object to an *objet d'art*, an object with a perceived artistic value.

Take the recent plastic-case radio collecting craze. Radio collectors consider these radios common. Many ignore them completely. Catalin and other phenolic case radios are priced in the radio category in *Warman's Americana & Collectibles*, third edition, by color: $25 to $35 for one with a black case, $50 to $150 for a red case, and $150 to $300 for a blue case. A number of veteran radio collectors shake their heads in disgust even at these prices.

Market manipulators and entrepreneurs outside the radio collecting fraternity have turned plastic-case radios into *objets d'art.* A large number of collectors and museums have fallen for their ploy. Philip Collins's *Radios: The Golden Age* (Chronicle Books, 1987) is the movement's bible. The radios are photographed to emphasize their design element. The photography is gorgeous, the printing superb. Thumbing through the book almost makes me want to drool.

Collins's photographs make one forget that the case was merely a window dressing to hide the works. Judging radios in this context is like judging a person solely by physical appearance. Have we forgotten the essentials?

Collins's presentation tends to treat each radio equally. He offers no standards by which to differentiate one radio design from another. A concept of universal goodness is necessary for successful market manipulation. It allows the manipulators to put a high price tag on everything.

Please do not infer from what I have said that I think collectibles lack aesthetic quality. Quite the contrary. Many collectibles exhibit a high aesthetic quality through their design or the image that they convey. Giovanni Fanelli and Ezio Godoli's *Art Nouveau Postcards* (Rizzoli International Publications, 1987) perfectly illustrates this point. Fanelli and Godoli rely on the postcards themselves to show the tremendous diversity of the Art Nouveau moment throughout Europe and the United States. The presentation is an educational and visual feast. The authors also deserve praise for their excellent introduction, well worth reading by anyone interested in collecting postcards, and thorough biographical dictionary of postcard artists and illustrators.

Now that I have covered the manipulative approach and touched briefly on the scholarly-aesthetic approach, what about the "Just for the Fun of It" approach. Hats off to Abbeville Press. Whoever convinced Abbeville to emphasize the fun side of collectibles deserves a place in collectors' heaven. If you do not own a copy of Gideon Bosker's *Great Shakes: Salt and Pepper for All Tastes* (Abbeville Press, 1986), Rod Dryer and Ron Spark's *Fit to Be Tied: Vintage Ties of the Forties and Early Fifties* (Abbeville Press, 1987), or H. Thomas Steele, Jim Heimann, and Rod Dyer's *Close Cover Before Striking: The Golden Age of Matchbook Art* (Abbeville Press, 1987), buy a copy now. Of course, this admonition does not apply to museum curators. I would rather they stay ignorant of the potential artistic value of these three subject areas.

Bosker's book deserves special recognition because he demonstrates the pure joy that can be found in displaying collectibles. Far too many collectors place their objects on shelves, like good soldiers lining up for reveille. Bosker creates settings. I will never be able to look at another animal salt and pepper shaker set without visualizing his Noah's ark scene or vegetable set and thinking of the introductory photograph to the "Counter Culture" chapter.

While I like the organization of the match cover book, it lacks the pizzazz of the salt and pepper shaker book. The fault rests in two areas: (1) the limitation of the subject matter and (2) the book's layout. It has none of the freedom and excitement of presentation found in *Great Shakes*.

Many critics of collectibles label them as kitsch. One need only point to *Fit to Be Tied* to support this theory. As a young man, I wore ties similar to the ones pictured. They are my cultural and social heritage. Does this finally explain why I turned out as I did?

I do not believe that collectibles are kitsch. This is an argument of the "blue noses" to justify their own expensive brand of goodies. Collectibles are historical documents, the survivors that future generations will turn to in order to understand the time in which we live. If they occasionally show we exercised bad taste, so be it. No society is perfect. We preserve plenty of bad taste from past centuries.

Finally, I want to share a secret with you: Henry I. Kurtz and Burtt R. Ehrlich's *The Art of the Toy Soldier* (Abbeville Press, 1987). I love lead figures, soldier or civilian. They are mobile, even when stationary. Your mind moves them as you look at them. Kurtz and Ehrlich have created lifelike settings for their figures. If you are going to deal with collectibles as *objets d'art*, *The Art of the Toy Soldier* is how it should be done. Kudos also for the background information. *The Art of the Toy Soldier* is a perfect blend of text and photographs. It is not a coffee-table book, it is an adventure.

Controlling Value: The Hoard

COLLECTIBLES, twentieth-century mass-produced objects, are rarely one of a kind. If there is one, there is another, and another, and another. For this reason, the collector must constantly fear the discovery of a hoard, a large collection of identical objects that, when released into the market, significantly affect the object's desirability and price. A hoard gluts the market. In legal parlance, it is known as the "blockage effect."

A hoard does not have to be a large quantity to affect a collecting category. Usually ten to twenty items are enough, especially if they are top pieces and still in unused (excellent) condition. Many collecting categories have only a few key collectors at the top. Once their needs are satisfied, the price structure for that object is no longer valid.

The term "mass-produced" usually conjures up an image of a factory assembly line churning out thousands of cars, candy bars, or toys. What many people do not realize is that many craftspeople also mass-produced their wares. As such, their products must not be viewed as unique objects, but merely as utilitarian items made as quickly and cheaply as possible.

I encountered an excellent example of this when I attended the sale of the remnants of the Stahl family pottery in Powder Valley, Pennsylvania. For those unfamiliar with Stahl pottery, the family consisted of three generations of twentieth-century redware potters. They still fired their wares in a wood kiln. Folklorists and collectors have glorified the Stahls as the last redware potters in a tradition extending back to America's founding.

When I looked at the pottery for sale, I was struck by the large quantity of similar items. The folklorist image of the potter sitting at the wheel carefully crafting each pot was not true in the Stahl's case. The quantity of material actually revealed that the Stahls poured slip into molds to make as many cats, inkwells, etc., as they could in as short an amount of time as possible. They cranked it out.

When they weren't pouring slip, they were mass producing plates by slamming redware slabs over molds or making a hundred lids at a time for future pots or jar bases. The Stahl family pottery was a small scale factory. Any collector who elevates Stahl pieces to the level of American folk art is doing himself a major disservice.

Hoards are discovered all the time. Collectors follow closely the sale advertisements for old grocery and country stores, pharmacies, and warehouses. Dealers are constantly writing to manufacturers asking to buy discontinued merchandise and advertising material, especially if it relates to a current collecting fad. Finally, there are those foresighted individuals who buy a quantity of material when it is first produced, store it for ten to thirty years, and finally release it into the market.

How do you spot a hoard? The first clue is the sudden appearance of an item that you have not seen for years. If you notice the same item being offered for sale by a number of dealers at a collectibles show or in the trade papers, be suspicious. A person who finds a hoard usually tries to sell the objects to a variety of dealers throughout the country. In this way, a regional market is not glutted.

My recent purchase of a yellow vinyl Hopalong Cassidy child's shoe holder illustrates this point well. I have collected Hopalong Cassidy memorabilia for close to two decades. During that time I had acquired a red vinyl child's shoe holder, but I had never seen one in yellow. Suddenly one appeared in Hake's Americana & Collectibles mail auction. Within a week, a Texas dealer offered another one for sale through his ad in a trade paper. The condition of both pieces was excellent.

Condition is the second clue in identifying a hoard. When objects are found in a hoard, they generally are unused. Remember the source of the hoard — stores, warehouses, and discontinued merchandise. If anything is damaged, it is likely to be the packaging. When I see an object that is water-stained or mildewed, but otherwise in good condition, I immediately think of a hoard. This is storage damage, not damage from use.

Finding several identical objects in excellent to mint condition also may be a clue that a reproduction or newly manufactured product has been designed to take advantage of a sudden surge in prices in a collecting category. The way to differentiate between a hoard and these latter two groups is to thoroughly know the objects in your collecting area. Study product catalogs and visit museums and private collections until you know what products were made originally.

Relying on price to spot a hoard is difficult. Often the person who finds a hoard carefully controls the initial input into the market, charging a high price for the first few examples to test the market and quickly recover the initial outlay. If you see an unusual, excellent-condition object that is highly overpriced, place yourself on alert. If you see an unusual, excellent-condition object that is underpriced, suspect a hoard immediately.

A hoard can be too big. What does a dealer do if he has five hundred to a thousand examples of an object? There is no collectibles collecting category that is strong enough to absorb that many examples of a single object at one time. If the dealer is wise, he probably will destroy all but fifty to a hundred of the examples.

The ideal hoard size is about twenty to forty examples. The owner can control how the material enters the market and maintain a high price level. Enough examples exist to satisfy the demands of both the dealers and collectors.

A hoard has two principal effects on the market. In the long run, it significantly lowers the desirability and price for that object. In the collectibles field, desirability and availability are key elements in determining price. In fact, in many cases they outweigh design and aesthetic considerations. Collectible collectors want to possess examples that no other collector owns. When an object is available to everyone, it becomes common. There is little prestige in owning it.

Finally, a hoard has value only if it pertains to objects not already available in the market. If a hoard of fifty Hopalong Cassidy china dinner plates appeared on the market, the average selling price for such plates would change little. There already are more than enough plates on the market now to fill the collectors' demands.

The hoard is endemic to collectibles. As long as a collector is aware of it, the problem will remain minor.

✍

Fading Away

DURING a recent seminar I gave on the collectibles market, I became acutely aware that many of the participants did not recognize the personalities associated with a number of cartoon, movie, and radio items from the first half of the twentieth century that I used as illustrations. Among those who did not ring a bell were William Hart, Lum and Abner, and the Yellow Kid. As example after example appeared on the screen, I was reminded of General MacArthur's famous quote: "Old soldiers never die, they just fade away."

When memory fades completely, what happens to the value of a collectible associated with that memory? Fifty years from now will *Star Wars* collectibles be worth more or less than they are today? There is a strong possibility that "less" will prove the correct answer.

Nostalgia plays an important role in valuing collectibles. Many individuals begin collecting because they are trying to buy back a part of their childhood or youth. Collecting provides a means of escape from admitting that they are getting old.

A recent shift in collecting emphasis in the World's Fair category illustrates this point. In the late 1960s and early 1970s, the strongest collecting interest centered on the 1893 Columbian Exposition held in Chicago. A book was written that concentrated solely on the collectibles from this World's Fair.

My grandfather attended the 1893 Columbian Exposition as a young man.

His trip was a "grand" adventure, recounted by him with enthusiasm to whomever would listen. The stoneware mug that he brought home as a souvenir, now part of my collection, served as a constant reminder of the trip. Now, few remember and only a small number of collectors focus on the 1893 Columbian Exposition. It is a memory that has almost totally faded away.

The attention of the World's Fair collectors has shifted to the 1939 New York World's Fair. People remember it. The Trylon and Perisphere symbolized the dawning of a new age. Developing collector interest in modernistic pieces from the 1940s and 1950s, much of which was previewed at the 1939 New York World's Fair, has caused the price of 1939 New York World Fair collectibles to double in the past two years. Additional increases are likely.

People frequently ask me to explain the difference between an antique and collectible. Perhaps the answer is far more simple than most experts realize. A collectible is something associated with an event or time period that a majority of the population can still remember; an antique is something associated with an event or time period that most people have forgotten. If this is true, the date when something becomes classified as an antique keeps moving forward. Is it safe to say that anything made before 1930 or 1935 should now be classified as an antique? I think a strong argument can be made for this.

We have all heard the cry of the program seller at sporting events: "You can't tell the players without a scorecard." The collectible version is: "You can't value a collectible until you know to whom it refers." If you found a pot metal pin cushion of a smiling, childlike figure with large protruding ears and bald head dressed in a loosely fitting robe with "I'm Weightin For Yer See" in raised letters, how would you value it? As a figural pin cushion its value is in the $45 to $65 range. As a Yellow Kid collectible, its value is in the $150-plus range.

Have you ever wondered why collectible collectors do well when playing Trivial Pursuit? The answer is simple. They know the trivial details of the past. The "past" is not the past of a hundred years ago or longer, but the decades of the first half of the twentieth century.

It's time for a quiz. How many of the following twenty-five cartoon, movie, radio, or television characters can you identify by medium and time: Sergeant Bilko, Mr. Bluster, Major Bowes, Brownies, Buttercup, Ella Cinders, Denny Dimwit, Uncle Fester, Gracie, Andy Gump, Happy Hooligan, Humphrey, Buck Jones, Kayo, Kuryakin, Jerry Mahoney, My Little Margie, Mary Marvel, Fibber McGee, Red Ryder, Mortimer Snerd, Spark Plug, Toonerville, Captain Video, and Winnie Winkle? You pass if you get ten out of twenty-five. If you fail, its time to head for your local library and do a little reading about the twentieth century. You might be surprised how much you missed while you were growing up.

In every century there are giants whose collectibles always retain value. The twentieth-century list contains such celebrities as Amos and Andy, the Beatles, Charlie Chaplin, Hopalong Cassidy, Marilyn Monroe, Elvis Presley, Superman, Tarzan, and Shirley Temple. While you probably can add several others to this list, the key point is that the list is not endless. Name recognition is the key.

When someone tells me they have a letter signed by a member of Congress or by an important government official from the early part of the twentieth century, my first comment is: "Who has heard of him or remembers him?" If the answer is no one, then you have to question the potential value of the document.

A strong argument can be made that the more you know about something, the greater its collecting value. Research does add value. Clearly identifying a collectible with a key personality or character enhances its value. But be careful. Don't become so fascinated with the amount of information known that you assign too high a value. Ask yourself if the character or individual is well remembered. If memories have faded, so does a portion of the object's value.

I wish there were a way to stop the fading process. All we can hope is that there will always be enough collectors to keep those individuals and characters on my endangered species list from becoming totally extinct.

Who's Ed Wynn?

RECENTLY I received a letter from a reader asking for information about an Ed Wynn Texaco fireman's hat. I turned the research over to a young journalism major from Lehigh University, my alma mater, who I had hired for the summer. She took the letter and started. Ten minutes later she was standing sheepishly in front of my desk. The question she had to ask was basic, "Who's Ed Wynn?"

Now, this was not her major faux pas of the summer. During the course of interviewing her for the summer position, I told her that I was working on a book about Hopalong Cassidy. Not wanting to embarrass herself, she waited until she went home to ask her father who Hopalong Cassidy was. His answer was simple. Hopalong Cassidy was a running back for the Ohio State University football team. Her father was a Buckeye graduate. His answer reflects the shallowness of educational awareness fostered by that institution.

When she returned to work, she asked me about my interest in football, which, while considerable, cannot match my interest in Hopalong Cassidy. She was puzzled about why someone involved in antiques and collectibles would be working on a biography of an Ohio State football player.

The young woman has completed half her senior year. She completed the requisite courses in history and other social-science areas that are necessary for her training as a journalist. She has written for the campus paper for over a year. During her interview she showed an awareness of television and movie personalities from her era.

But here is the rub—"her era." Born in the early 1960s, her era of consciousness begins in the late 1960s, long after Ed Wynn and Hopalong Cassidy had vanished from the movie and television screens. Dwight Eisenhower, the Korean War, and yellow polka-dot bikinis—they are only abstractions to her.

As a refuge from the world of academe, I can understand why the young woman's education is so incomplete. I taught history at the college level. The courses focused on great political figures and broad social, intellectual, and high-level cultural currents. In an American history survey, there was so much to cover that if one made it to the end of World War II, one considered the course successful. Forget the last thirty years. Leave something for future historians to interpret.

Rarely do the history books or the history teachers look beyond the great academic questions and considerations to ask what really influenced the lives of "common" men. What shaped their version of truth, justice, and the American way? From what did they derive their standards of the "good life?" Who made the people laugh and cry?

As a collector, perhaps I realize more than most of the academic historians the powerful role played by the movies, radio, television, and other media in shaping the lives and expectations of each succeeding generation of Americans. I handle the mementos they left behind—the Captain Midnight decoder ring, the silver bullet, and the $64,000 Question TV game.

I do not think I was a movie, radio, or television junkie. But I went and I watched and I dreamed. Yes, dreamed that someday I would enjoy the life-style and respect accorded to Dr. William Todhunter Hall (Ronald Coleman) in "The Halls of Ivy," have the childhood of Andy Hardy (Mickey Rooney) and Henry Aldrich (Jackie Cooper; Jimmy Lydon), the madness of Spike Jones, and the humor of Ed Wynn and Milton Berle.

Why has academic history ignored the Ed Wynns of the world? The great entertainers have influenced us as much, if not more, than many of the political and social figures found in the textbooks. The great entertainers are important historical personalities of their time and they deserve recognition.

We have special cable stations for news, sports, tele-evangelism, home auction sales, and a variety of other functions. A great opportunity exists for someone to develop a cable station that features movies that influenced the generations born before 1960. I am not talking about the great film classics that academic film historians adore, such as *Citizen Kane* and *High Noon*. I am talking about films that feature Eddie Cantor, Bing Crosby, Marilyn Monroe, and other greats and near-greats of the entertainment past. The station might also feature reruns of the classic early television shows—"Life with Father," "Dragnet," and "My Little Margie" (Gale Storm). I've had it with reruns of "Hogan's Heroes," " Laverne and Shirley," and "M.A.S.H."

If the modern young adults were exposed to such a station, they might achieve a far greater understanding of their parents than reading about the civil rights marches of the 1960s. But my motives are not solely altruistic. Quite honestly, they are rather mercenary. How will we be able to convince anyone to buy an Ed Wynn Texaco fireman's hat if they do not know who Ed Wynn is?

My biggest fear is that many of the new younger collectibles dealers, the ones getting their start this summer at flea markets across the country, enjoy the same ignorance of the pre-1960 period as does my summer employee. Unless they understand why and for whom the games, toys, and other mementos of the past were produced, they will treat them as abstract objects with only a financial value.

Collectibles have stories to tell—why were they made, who made them, how were they marketed, who owned them, why were they saved, and why someone is buying them now. What good are they without these stories? Collectibles are not things to be worshiped, they are things to be loved.

Ed Wynn deserves to be more than a footnote in history, a question in a trivia game. Ed Wynn deserves to be remembered. Ed Wynn was "The Perfect Fool." Post-1960 baby boomers—get off your duff and learn about the past. Otherwise, we'll be using the same phrase for you, but in an entirely different context.

Part 4
Understanding the Collector

What Kind of Collector Are You?

I think it is possible to divide every collectibles category into three basic groups of material: common items, hard-to-find items, and rare items. A collector type is associated with each group. Common items are associated with the casual collector and cross-category collector; hard-to-find items with the serious collector; and rare items with the dedicated collector or "nut."

Common items constitute the greatest bulk of any collectibles category. While hundreds of articles have been written about collectibles, almost no one has ever done research on how many items were produced in a given category. Remember, when I think "collectible," I think in terms of thousands to millions.

I am currently doing research for a book about the character of Hopalong Cassidy, played in film and on television by William Boyd. To my delight, I am being given access to the endorsement contracts that Boyd signed for many of the products that bear his picture, name, and/or logo. At best, I'll have a conservative idea of the number of items made. But I expect the numbers to be higher than most collectors in the past have predicted.

The truth of the matter is that probably seventy to eighty percent of the material in any collectible category falls in the common realm. Dealers and collectors have a tendency to make things rarer than they are. I feel the burden of proof should be on them to prove that they are hard to find or rare.

Common items constitute the core of any collection. Once collectors have assembled a sufficiently large collection of this type of material, they have to make a basic decision. Do they go on or rest content with their stash?

The casual collector and cross-category collector drop out at his point. The casual collector has enough material to satisfy the nostalgia fix. Cross-category collectors, who buy only because an item may relate to their major collecting category, have better things in mind on which to spend their money.

Two key observations must be made. The casual collector probably constitutes between sixty and seventy percent of any collecting category. There are simply not as many serious collectors and dedicated collectors as we usually think.

Casual collectors also rarely want more than one example of an object. They don't need two. No Hopalong Cassidy collector that I know about wants a place setting for eight of the Hopalong Cassidy breakfast china set.

Assembling the core collection is both fun and usually inexpensive. Nothing applies the brakes to the casual collector's interest in a category faster than having to pay higher and higher prices to obtain the hard-to-find and rare objects needed to continue a collection.

Collecting is fad-related. A category gets a shot in the arm when new collectors rush in. Unfortunately, the rush is always sporadic. When each new group of collectors in a category has assembled its core collections, the market in that category dries up.

Hard-to-find items constitute twenty-five to thirty percent of the market and are sought only by the serious collector. Serious collectors, with their ability to sustain their collecting interests over several decades, are patient and persistent. They know what objects exist within their collecting category and have determined how they will obtain them.

Serious collectors organize collectors' clubs, research and write about their category, and establish museums. They share their information quite willingly in hopes of gaining leads to new material and attracting more individuals to their collecting interest.

Serious collectors, however, work within narrow parameters. They want only one example of an object, just like casual collectors. They want the best example possible. So, often they will sell a lesser example to obtain a better example and upgrade their collections.

There is a limit to how much they are willing to spend. Serious collectors always have financial constraints in mind. They usually have their collecting enthusiasm well under control.

Personally, I would like to see the words "rare" and "scarce" dropped from the vocabulary of both the antiques and collectibles field. I do recognize that there are a limited number of objects, perhaps ten to twenty in each collectibles category, of which only a few examples exist.

It is the dedicated collector or "nut" who seeks these rare objects. He or she is possessed with one simple burning desire—to own an example of every item in that category. Price is no limit; no distance is too far to travel.

The dedicated collector makes up less than five percent of the collectors in any collectibles category. In fact, I contend that any collectibles category is dominated by a group of less than ten individuals at the top. In many cases, this number is five or less.

The identification of these "top dollar" collectors is among the best-kept secrets in the collectibles field. The collectors themselves prefer anonymity. They frequently communicate with each other. But they constitute a closed circle that admits a new member only after careful scrutiny.

In summary, I am trying to make two points. First, the vast majority of objects in any collectibles category are common rather than hard to find or rare. Second, the number of buyers in any collectibles is relatively small compared to the large number of objects that have survived.

Casual collectors probably number less than two hundred, serious collectors less than fifty, and dedicated collectors less than ten in any collectibles category.

Specialization in collecting makes the collectibles market far more narrow than many realize. There's only one thing to do that makes sense. Let's get out there and turn on some more people. We need them.

Packrats of America

I make no bones about it. I have crossed that thin line that separates the collector from the accumulator. A collector is defined in *Webster's* as "one who makes a collection." Note the use of the singular form for "collection," not the plural. Collectors are single-focused. Their collecting may require that they obtain objects from other collecting categories, but their focus is truly singular.

An accumulator makes a collection of collections. An accumulator's mission is simple — save as many things as humanly possible. Never once is the accumulator overwhelmed by the task. The goal is attainable. While his efforts are certain to achieve him sainthood in the collecting fraternity, the animosity he encounters from spouse and children certainly precludes his enjoying his heavenly rewards on earth.

Nostalgia is one of the principal motivations for the collector. Not true for the accumulator. The accumulator saves many objects that evoke no recollections of childhood, grandmother, or apple pie. Why? What motivates the accumulator?

The key concept is "neat." The accumulator collects neat things. He may justify his saving tendency with excuses such as "It's too good to throw out," "Someone ought to save it," or "I'll eventually find a good home for it," but behind all these phrases is the fact that the accumulator saved it because it was neat.

Neat things present problems. There is no museum to leave them to. Often there is no resale market. No one writes books or price guides about neat things. What is neat to one accumulator is often not neat to another.

Accumulators should not be confused with junk collectors. Junk is second-hand, worn, or discarded articles of little value and meaning. Accumulators are quite willing to spend a great deal of money building their accumulations. I know. I apply the same criteria to buying my neat things as I do when buying my antiques and collectibles.

How do you classify accumulators? Several months ago I received a letter from a reader in Valley Stream, New York. She might have hit the nail on the head by identifying accumulators as packrats.

> I want to plead the case for better attention to a genre that might be called Packrats of America. We have no associations, no chapters, no conventions, not even a newsletter. Chances are we do not even know the fellow packrat down the block, until his driveway blossoms out into a garage sale.
>
> More attention should be paid to us, because we are the custodians of collectibles that stand in peril of being lost forever. Of course, some of us have valuable antiques, but these will eventually find their way to the market. Our significance lies in the small stuff. In our collective attics and basements we have custody of thousands of collectibles that, without some intelligent intervention, will someday find themselves relegated to the trash heap by our less tradition-oriented, unpackrat-like heirs and assigns.
>
> For example, I am a sixty-five-year-old, third-generation packrat. In addition to the odd legacies from my predecessor packrats, I am driven by congenital packratmania to rescue old things threatened with extinction if they do not sell at a garage sale or similar event. I do not actually want them, but I am certain someone, somewhere does, and I cannot see them destroyed.
>
> Other items have been left, like waifs, in my hands because others refuse to either throw them away or keep them. They know I am a patsy.
>
> As a consequence, although I do collect some things, I am also an accumulator of odd bits and pieces of collectibles that I do not really want.
>
> I do not collect Railroadiana, but I have a World War II Chesapeake and Ohio poster showing "Chessie" in army gear, a 1911 railroad timetable of Sunday Seashore Excursions from Augusta, Georgia, and some Pennsylvania Railroad calendars from the 1950s.

I do not collect postcards but have some four hundred of them, with several dating as early as 1909. I will bet somebody somewhere wants a 1916 bird's-eye view of Houston Street in San Antonio or a 1916 picture of the *New Yorker,* a New York City fireboat. But whom?

I do not collect Black memorabilia, but I have a 1914 edition of Marion F. Harmon's *Negro Wit and Humor,* a relic of the "darkie" days.

The list goes on and on.

I am not above selling some things, but dickering with dealers is not on my agenda. When they ask me to set a price, I do not know what to say.

I could go dump the whole collection of postcards with a dealer for a few dollars. However, I would get a lot more fun out of finding the specialist who yearns for that fireboat and just giving it to him or swapping for some Tuck postcards.

A way must be found to open a channel between the collectors and the packrats. Can you help?

The Founder and Only Member of Packrats of America

One solution suggested by the founder of Packrats of America is to have one or more of the major trade papers develop a swap column patterned after the one that was featured in the now-defunct *Collectibles Illustrated.* Perhaps for a modest fee of three to five dollars, a person could run a four-or-five line ad offering to swap what they have for something else. The tradition of swapping has always been an important method of passing things from one collector to another, but it has never been formalized.

There must be other solutions. What are your thoughts. Send your suggestions to: Rinker on Collectibles, P.O. Box 248, Zionsville, PA 18092.

Meanwhile, I have a suggestion for my Valley Stream, New York, reader. Fear not. If your heirs and assigns do not want your stuff, I am available for adoption.

Things My Daddy Never Told Me

COLLECTIBLES are sexist. It's true. There are things collected principally by men; there are things collected principally by women. You would think the Age of Aquarius and Women's Liberation would have changed things. Fat chance. Collecting is a conservative bastion, a place where "tradition" has real meaning.

Strangely enough, it was being a member of the Hellertown–Lower Saucon High School band that first called my attention to the sexist nature of things. The next time you have an opportunity, watch a high school marching band. Are the majority of the clarinet and flute players female? Are the majority of trumpet and tuba players male? It was not until I went to Lehigh University, an all-male institution at the time, that I realized that males actually played the flute.

A recent announcement that I received from the Franklin Mint again piqued my thinking about the sexism of collectibles. In "The Franklin Mint Fact Sheet—1988" was the following information about the Product Marketing Divisions:

> The Franklin Mint's products are conceived, designed and executed under the aegis of four distinct marketing divisions:
>
> ☞ *Female Collectibles.* The single largest segment of the Company's business, this area includes heirloom dolls; hand-crafted sculpture in various mediums; reproductions of original works of art from prestigious museums and eclectic collections.
>
> ☞ *Male Collectibles.* Major product lines include die-cast replicas of famous automobiles; dramatic porcelain sculpture; collectible board games and fine weapon replicas. . . .

The Franklin Mint's approach to collectibles shows a keen understanding of the market. They are light-years ahead of most collectors and dealers.

Museums provide excellent examples of the hidden sexism that can be conveyed through the presentation of antiques and collectibles. The vast majority of museum curators are women. When they set up period rooms, the rooms have a distinct female flavor, from the choice of colors for furnishings and draperies to the accessories found on tables and dressers.

While I was executive director of the Historical Society of York County (Pennsylvania), I instructed my preparator, who was male, to revise one of the period rooms and give it a distinctly male flavor. I did not ask the permission of the museum committee, which was controlled by a group of hard-core female traditionalists. The preparator did an excellent job. The Federal-period room had the appearance of home to a forty-year-old bachelor with minimum housekeeping skills. I loved it. The furor it created was equivalent to Point 7 on the Richter scale.

In the late 1960s *Spinning Wheel,* a sorely missed collector's magazine that dealt with middle-range antiques and collectibles, sold a series of books that recognized the sexist nature of collecting. Louis H. Hertz's *Antique Collecting for Men* (Galahad, 1969) pointed out that men were the dominant market force in categories such as firearms, lead soldiers, toys, and western memorabilia.

The environment in which we live shapes our sexual perceptions. Collections often are an extension of these views. I suspect I am as good a representative as any. Although an eclectic accumulator of the first order, I certainly own far more Hopalong Cassidy memorabilia than I do dolls, far more dimestore soldiers than I do dimestore civilians, and far more fast-food collector glasses with superheroes than with Peanuts characters.

When Harold Nichols sent me a copy of his *McCoy Cookie Jars: From the First to the Latest* (Nichols Publishing, 1987), he also sent me a copy of Mike Chapman's *Nick and the Cyclones* (Leisure Press, 1988). Harold Nichols was head wrestling coach at Iowa State University from 1953 to 1985. His Iowa State Cyclones were a man's-man team. Viewing Harold as a leading authority on McCoy cookie jars, traditionally a female collectible, requires a different mind-set. Harold's own actions suggest that even he is a bit defensive.

No doubt the liberation and sexual revolutions of the 1960s and 1970s will produce changes in the antiques and collectibles field. Most flea markets now feature unisex toilets. Are unisex collectibles next? I certainly hope not. If the threat occurs, I personally will lead the fight against them. I see nothing wrong with the sexism of collectibles.

And now for the final, ultimate, ugly truth: The antiques and collectibles field is female-dominant, especially in the middle- and low-end sector. Go to any antiques and collectibles flea market, mall, or show. Count the number of male dealers and the number of female dealers. Visit the bookseller. Count the number of collectibles books written by women and then by men. Men, we are the minority.

Look at the most prevalent male collecting areas: baseball cards, firearms, toys, transportation (railroad, steamship, and toy trains) memorabilia, and sports collectibles. These are not things that you would find at the ordinary antiques and collectibles flea market, mall, or show. Men have created their own show circuits for each of these specialties.

Much of male collecting is underground. You hear little about it. It is done at night on the telephone. Wives are never informed. Men may know about their wives' collections, but not vice versa. It is a shame the IRS is not a little mouse.

At this point, I suspect that you will think that I will get out my soap-box and raise a hue and cry that would result in more men widening their collecting interest and role in all aspects of the antiques and collectibles field. Nothing of the sort. I want to sing the praises of the women who made collecting and dealing in antiques and collectibles the respectable hobby and occupation that it has become today.

The antiques and collectibles business is labor intensive. It is hard work and low pay. It is dealing with others with a friendly smile and the ability to hold one's temper in check. It is persistence and dedication. It is paying dues that extend for decades, not for months or years. It is something women seem more willing to do than men.

When I was attending Hellertown–Lower Saucon High School in the 1950s, I joined the Future Teachers of America. Why? Simple. I was the only male in this otherwise female organization. Men, do not become the dominant force in the antiques and collectibles field. Don't ruin the good thing that I have going.

My Favorite Piece

WHILE I was appearing on a radio show recently, the interviewer asked what seemed to be a rather simple question. ""What's your most favorite piece in your collection?"

Normally, I always have a ready reply to any question I am asked. But, this question made me pause.

My first reaction was to answer, "I don't have a single favorite piece." This response ducked the question and provided an easy way out. I should have taken it.

Instead, I thought back to my home and office, where stacks of boxes and drawers are filled with the diversity of my collecting manias: Hopalong Cassidy, charge tokens and credit cards, comic books, political buttons, games, quilts, Pennsylvania Dutch material, postcards, shopping bags. The list is endless. In truth, I am the true eclectic, eccentric collector.

If disaster struck and I could save only one object from the totality of my collections, which one would I save? The very thought surpasses the horror of Frankenstein or the fear of Hell. That interviewer's question gave me nightmares.

The dedicated collector doesn't have a favorite item. We have favorites, plural! Worst yet, we love them all.

The more I think about it, the more convinced I become that single objects merge into a unified whole and lose their identity in the mind of the dedicated collector.

The collection is the all-controlling force that dominates our lives. Everything is related to everything else. Objects are viewed only in their relationship to other objects.

I sat back and thought about the great collectors I know. One individual came immediately to mind.

He was afflicted with a love affair with cars, acquired during his boyhood. His first acquisition was an old Chevy. As he prospered, he branched out into vintage cars.

When space and storage became a major consideration, he switched to scale models and miniatures, as well as assembling a toy collection of tin, lead, cast-iron, and plastic automobiles, trucks, fire engines, and even trains.

The next collecting phase saw him branch out into automobile memorabilia, ranging from giveaway premiums from manufacturers and dealers to match safes embossed with an automobile. If it had to do with automobiles or had a picture of an automobile on it, he wanted it.

By now his collecting obsession was the major focus of his life. His days, nights, and weekends revolved around buying. His collection expanded to include automobile art, lithographs, oil paintings, posters, porcelains, and sculpture.

He ran out of space again. He built more rooms, creating his own personal museum where he could browse among the sum total of his collectibles. When he ran out of this new space, he added another room and more display cases.

At this point, something happened. The mania was still there. But the original sex appeal and chemistry began to lag. It was getting harder and harder and more and more expensive to find exciting new material.

While still faithful to his original mistress, he now is embarking on a new romance—a collection of baseball memorabilia. This is dedication. This is craziness.

But could he name his favorite automobile piece? No way! Absolutely not! Everything in the collection is precious to him.

I was back to square one. How to answer the darn question?

I have met people who are in love with one specific antique or collectible.

Almost without fail, they are a casual dilettante collector, not a dedicated collector. Like the Sunday painter, the dilettante collects on a whim, buys on impulse (a few dollars here, a few dollars there), and shies away from making a commitment to assembling a meaningful collection. They are trendy and willing to shift allegiance to a collecting category the minute their current interest becomes unfashionable.

What they want more than anything from the antiques and collectibles they own is bragging rights. We need these persons in the market, but we don't have to like them. So much for this approach.

Then, I had an inspiration and the answer became crystal clear. What's my favorite piece?

Why, the next one, of course.

Knee Deep in . . .

WHILE working on a recent column, I needed something that I had stored in a shoe box on the player piano located in front of the fireplace at my office. I asked one of my employees to get it for me. She stared in disbelief. "What player piano?" she asked. The employee was new, so I casually dismissed her remark until a second employee, who has worked with me for over a year, exclaimed, "You have a player piano?"

I was shocked. Could things possibly be so bad that the assortment of boxes and bags stored on, under, and around my player piano had totally disguised what it was? Admittedly, I begin about three to five new collections a month while continuing to add to those I started earlier, but surely I had not become so obsessed that I had allowed the sheer volume of material to become so overwhelming that it was destroying my living and working environment. It was time for an honest assessment.

I became painfully aware as I walked around my office that the space available for walking seemed to be confined to narrow aisles, each side of which contained layer upon layer of shoe, clothing, stationery, and other boxes. I was knee-deep in goodies. No longer was there any doubt; I had crossed that fine line that separates the collector from the accumulator.

I gave the matter some thought. Instinctively, I placed the blame on Grandpop Prosser. He was the ideal accumulator role model. Grandpop Prosser was one of those individuals who picked up bent nails from the street, carried them home, straightened them out, sorted them by size, and waited until the time arose when he might need them. He saved everything. By the time I got to know him well, his boxes were shoulder-high and occupied his basement and several rooms of the house.

Each box was a treasure chest. You never knew what was in it. The collection ran from scraps of wood, to a vast array of watch parts, to sexology magazines, to Ku Klux Klan literature. Grandpop Prosser's interests were truly eclectic. The wonderful thing about Grandpop was that, although his boxes contained no labels, he seemed to know exactly where everything was. I think I was one of the few individuals among his children and grandchild that truly appreciated the magnificence of what he had assembled.

If my parents were alive, I am certain they would attest to the fact that whatever gene drove Grandpop Prosser to collect was also inherited by me. I have collected as far back as I can remember. It seemed such a natural part of life.

I may have made a fatal error when I chose a career that encouraged this madness. Two recent events finally drove me over the edge. Immediately after the first edition of *Warman's Americana & Collectibles* was published, I decided to collect one object from every category in the book. I have fewer than twenty-five categories to go to complete the project. If I could only find room for the jukebox and pinball, slot, and vending machines, I would pass my last major hurdles.

However, it was Shirley Swaab who opened the flood gates when she asked me to prepare a lecture on weird and strange things people collect. I fell in love with it all. A few examples from each category were not enough. Overnight, fifty new collections arose, ranging from things made out of animal parts to water pistols.

The problem with accumulating is that you have to store the stuff. My wife and employees cannot buy shoes and clothing fast enough to meet my storage demands. We do not eat lunch at the office anymore because the lunch table is filled with things waiting to be put in boxes. I no longer offer friends the use of the guest bed because it has so much stored on top of it that it would take several hours to relocate the goodies in order to provide sleeping accommodations. It is cheaper to pay for their hotel room or impose on my mother-in-law.

Accumulators probably should not be married, especially to another accumulator. When I met Connie, my wife, I thought I was safe. She swore that she did not collect. Alas, if it had only been true. Her cat collectibles, which I tried unsuccessfully to confine to the kitchen, have now filled her office/sewing room and are creeping out into the living room and television room. I do not blame her; I think she has caught the disease from me.

Today, society views alcoholism and gambling as a disease. Perhaps they should do the same for accumulating. We need to establish Collectors Anonymous, an organization that will maintain a hotline you can call each time you feel compelled to purchase another antique or collectible. We need to hold meetings where collectors can stand up and describe in gut-wrenching detail the things they did not buy at the latest show or flea market. This sounds sadistic to me.

Actually, I have found it safer simply to deny my affliction. At least once a day I assert that my collecting has not gotten the better of me. I still am in control. I can say no. I do not have to have one of everything. Does anyone have a warehouse they wish to rent? A garage will not work; there simply is not enough room.

Wait! There is still hope. I am only knee-deep in boxes. All I have to do is keep on stacking. What good is all that empty space between my knees and the ceiling? It ought to be used; it ought to serve some function. Waist level, here I come.

They're Organized out There

ONE of the reasons I love collectibles is the enthusiasm of the collectibles collectors. When was the last time you spoke with the Chief Croaker or received a letter signed "purringly yours?"

In the world of collectibles, the woofers, the oinkers, the hooters, and almost everyone else are organized into a plethora of national and regional collectors' clubs. These organizations are why the collectibles market has such vitality in today's antiques world.

Recently I attended the annual convention of the Rathkamp Matchcover Society; 398 people were registered. Individuals traveled from England, Australia, Canada, and behind the Iron Curtain to take part. While the convention technically began on a Wednesday and ended on a Saturday, most of the participants were at the convention hotel by Monday and heavily engaged in discussing and trading match covers.

Can you imagine 398 collectors of Queen Anne furniture gathering for a week to discuss the fine points of their collecting hobby? Why, there probably are not even 398 Queen Anne furniture collectors, discounting museums, in existence.

In the collectibles field, the collectors' club provides many essential services. In almost every instance, it issues a newsletter. Some are monthly, others quarterly. Each issue is filled with research and other information about the collectible that will never appear in general trade publications. The newsletter of the National Elephant Collectors' Society even contains an obituary column, outlined in black, for deceased zoo elephants.

Most newsletters include advertising or a swap column. Many collectors' clubs offer free advertising space in their publications as part of the membership fee. I always have contended that a great deal of the buying and selling of collectibles is among private individuals. Judging from the volume of advertising in collectors' club newsletters, I am correct.

Many collectors' clubs publish their membership list. You receive a copy when you join. It is usually revised annually. Think about this for a minute.

Suppose you had a large collection of games for sale. For fifteen dollars you can join the American Game Collectors Association. The moment you receive their membership list, you have access to the biggest game collectors in the country. Isn't the goal of every seller to reach the top buyer for his goods? Not a bad position to be in for a modest fifteen-dollar investment. If some free advertising is thrown in as part of the deal, so much the better.

But it is at their annual conventions that the collectors' clubs really shine. The spirit, the enthusiasm, and mania is nonstop. Information is exchanged willingly. Swapping is the order of the day, or week, with an occasional auction to enhance the madness of exchange.

It is important to understand that many collectors' clubs are subdivided into a wealth of smaller clubs. During the match cover convention, there were separate meetings of the International Club (specializing in hotel chains), the New Moon Club (matchbox collectors), the Girlies Club, and separate meetings of Jewel, Uniglow, and Foilite covers (all varieties of covers made by Universal Match Company). The International Club, New Moon Club, and Girlies Club have their own newsletters.

Collectors' club conventions provide an excellent opportunity to see material that generally is not on the market. Collectors love to show off and brag about their possessions. Many conventions feature a display room with exhibits that are judged and open to the public.

In the realm of collectibles, there is a collectors' club for just about everything. They range from broad-based clubs, such as the Ephemera Society and Federation of Historical Bottle Clubs, to specific clubs, such as the Pennsylvania Canal Society or the International Society of Animal License Collectors.

How do you find these collectors' clubs? The best source is the *National Avocation Organizations* annual directory, published by Columbia Books, Inc. (1350 New York Avenue, NW, Suite 207, Washington, D.C. 20005). It costs a modest $30.

The category introductions in *Warman's Americana and Collectibles* (Warman Publishing Company, 1985) list collectors' clubs for the categories included in that publication. *Wallace-Homestead's Price Guide to Antiques,* tenth edition (Wallace-Homestead, 1984), contains a list of collectors' clubs in the front matter.

A final source is Ralph and Terry Kovel's *The Kovel's Collectors' Source Book* (Crown Publishers, 1983), clearly my favorite collectibles reference tool, next to my own book. Even though it is slightly out of date, the information in it is indispensable to anyone involved with collectibles.

There is a sad note in this otherwise upbeat story about collectors' clubs. Many of them are rather short-lived. It is the exceptional club that survives for more than twenty-five years. Most are started by a few enthusiastic individuals who do all the work. When they have become tired of the responsibility, they frequently have trouble finding someone to take over.

But while collectors' clubs may vanish, the information they published does not. My reference files are filled with copies of *The Granitegram, The Milk Route, The Owl's Nest,* and similar publications. They are among my most valuable research tools.

Part 5
Research and Catalog Hints

Researching Collectibles: The Pluses and the Needs

ONE thing that differentiates the collectibles collectors from the antiques collectors is the amount of time they spend researching the history of the objects in their collection. Train collectors, for example, may know much more about their objects than do individuals who own eighteenth-century furniture, pewter, or redware.

Antiques collectors point to the lack of historical records to justify their lack of knowledge. For them, however, the lure of the hunt ending in the acquisition of an expensive piece is the true satisfying factor, not the research labor that adds significantly to the knowledge of the piece, its maker, or its user. They are lazy. They rely on art historians, museum curators, and antiquarians to do their research for them. Of course, there are exceptions to this generalization, but their number is few.

In stark contrast to the reliance on experts by the antiques collectors, most collectibles collectors strive to make themselves expert. Ask a breweriana collector from Allentown about the Horlacher or Neuweiler breweries and be prepared for a verbal dissertation that is likely to last for hours. Collectibles collectors willingly spend days and weeks tracing the history of the objects in their collection.

Collectibles collectors share their knowledge. Only a few zealously guard their research and try to keep it secret. Most freely share their information. Many do so only verbally; they are hesitant to put their results in writing. Others prepare articles for trade papers, pamphlets, and books.

The great tragedy is that much of the information that appears in the trade papers is lost. Few collectors cut out and file the articles. Most discard the papers when they are finished reading them. *The Antique Trader Weekly* used to prepare a yearly compendium of its articles. These compendia were among the most valuable research references in the field. Unfortunately, sales of the annual volumes were minimal, and *The Antique Trader Weekly* discontinued the practice.

Few of the trade papers are available on microfilm or microfiche. There is no major index to the articles of a single trade paper, let alone an index for all the papers in the field. My staff dreads the moments when I say, "I remember seeing an article about (blank) in one of the trade papers this past year. Find it."

Two recent events illustrate this point. I wanted to locate some information about eye-wash cups. I had remembered seeing an article about them in the trade paper within the past two years. Checking the files under eye-wash cups, medical, and pharmaceutical failed to turn up the clipped article. I was forced to retrace someone's previous research.

The second incident was far worse. I remembered a series of fake belt buckles that had inundated the collectibles market in the early 1970s. After a few had passed as originals, articles appeared in both the trade papers and collectors' club bulletins documenting the fakes. The time lapse was now over a decade, not a few years. The antiques and collectibles field has no central source that documents and publishes annual data on fakes and reproductions. Luckily I found some old-timers who had remembered seeing the fake buckles.

An opportunity exists for a publisher to serve collectors by offering annual compendia of the best articles about antiques and collectibles from the major trade papers or an annual article index. These publications are unlikely to make the publisher rich, but they will create many friends. A modern approach would be to enter these data on a computer and make them available through a modem or on a computer disk. Anyone up to the challenge?

I do not want to give the impression that everything we need to know has been discovered and inadvertently lost. Plenty of opportunities exist to do some exciting new research. This point was clearly demonstrated when I tried to find information about yo-yos and Sun Rubber Company toys.

When I was growing up, there were two major yo-yo companies—Duncan and Cheerio. Recently I acquired a box of Cheerio yo-yos and wanted to know more about the company. A search of all available literature produced nothing. The most recent books dated back to the late 1970s and, except for one, have a minimum of historical information. A call to the Buffalo and Erie County Historical Society and the Buffalo and Erie County Public Library in Buffalo and the Strong Museum in Rochester produced no results.

The Strong Museum, one of the country's major collectibles museums, wrote to say the museum did not even have a yo-yo in its collection. A letter from the Buffalo Public Library read: "Neither our Local History File nor the Buffalo Business File in our Business and Labor Department made any mention of the firm or its manager. There was also nothing indexed under the subject 'Yo-yos.' Apparently, the firm was short-lived and did not make a big impact on Buffalo's business community." Cheerio yo-yos short-lived? Not in my memory, or in that of many others who grew up in the 1930s through the 1950s.

Few children of the 1940s and early 1950s escaped playing with a Sun Rubber toy, usually an airplane, car, or truck with a Walt Disney character on it. When I acquired a toy truck from the Sun Rubber Company, I thought it would be a simple matter to turn to one of the many books on toys and find a history of the company. As you probably have guessed, I found nothing. Again, I pursued the subject, and through the kind efforts of the staff of the Barberton Public Library (Barberton, Ohio) was able to acquire the information I needed.

Whenever I handle a collectible, I ask myself who is the manufacturer, how was it made, for whom was it made, how was it merchandised, who acquired it, and why was it saved. The answers to these questions add personality to an object, a strong aspect of the collectible mystique.

Since collectibles are twentieth century in origin, the answers to these questions can still be found. The search is exciting. It can strain a marriage. Try telling your wife that the trip to Bermuda has been canceled in favor of a trip to Providence, Rhode Island, to interview a yo-yo player.

Serving as an advocate for antiques and collectibles is actually my third career. I was once part of the academic community and museum profession. What I have learned over the past decade is that preservers of the history of the common man (sorry—I simply cannot write "common person") are not the learned scholars, but the collectibles collectors. They are the ones who care enough to do the research about the things we lived with, played with, listened to, and watched. In time, they may leave us with a far better legacy of life in the twentieth century than all the Ph.D. dissertations combined.

You and Your Local Library

WHEN I ask dealers and collectors if they ever use their local library, I am amazed at how many answer no. I don't understand this because even though I have one of the largest reference libraries in the antiques and collectibles field, I constantly use my local library to supplement the material I have.

I don't have to tell anyone that the price of books about antiques and collectibles is on the increase. Finding a book today for under $10.95 is a rarity. In fact, prices in the $15 to $30 range are common. It costs several thousand dollars a year to maintain an adequate general reference library, let alone keeping up with the trade newspapers, magazines, and auction catalogs.

Your library can help. Books about antiques and collectibles are one of the most heavily used sections in local libraries. Librarians frequently will order a book for their collection if they think there will be sufficient demand. You'll be surprised, once you have established yourself as a regular user, how little persuasion is required to get a book you want.

Your library gives you a chance to preview a book before you buy it. Many books with attractive-sounding titles do not deliver the information you frequently need. If you are trying to find the price of something, the most detailed history or listing of pieces is useless unless there is a price guide. It is better to know this before you spend $25.

Your library also is a great source for out-of-print material. I am always amazed at how frequently my local Emmaus Public Library can find a book on its own shelves or within the Allentown library system, of which it is a part.

If your library doesn't have the book you need, ask them to find it for you through interlibrary loan. Usually the service is free. Sometimes a fee is involved, but it is a small price to pay for access to good information. Don't ask your librarian to do more than is necessary. Make certain you have the full name of the author, title, publisher, date of publication, and ISBN number when you request a title.

If you receive a book from interlibrary loan, remember that it comes from another library and often has a shorter loan period than your own library. Use of the book quickly and return it.

Borrowing books from the library also is helpful if you only need some of the information the book contains. Make a copy of the pertinent section on a local copy machine. Suppose you only need the information on ten pages and can make copies at 10¢ each. The cost is $1. Isn't this better than spending over $15 for the book. Make certain you understand the copyright laws thoroughly and, as a precaution, only make copies for your own use.

Thus far I have dealt with books. One of the principal reasons I use the library is for the magazines. Frankly, I don't subscribe to *The Magazine Antiques*. First, I think the subscription price is scandalous. Second, it rarely has articles that help me in my work. Third, I got tired of storing and hauling around piles of back issues. You can read it in the library for nothing. If you need information from some of the articles, there's always the copy machine. Check your local library to see what weekly or monthly publications in the antiques and collectibles field are part of their regular subscription list. Again, you can exert some influence about getting the material you need added to that list.

Don't forget those wonderful reference books that libraries maintain. There are reference books on collectors' societies, museums and historical societies, and many specialized subjects. One of the most valuable sources for me are national phone books. I always locate collectibles dealers in advance of going to a new area.

The wonderful thing about most public libraries is that all the services you receive are free. Oh, I realize that your tax dollars help support the library. However, if you are a heavy user or you are using the information to make money in your business, then you have an obligation to give something back. When the library has a building drive, make a donation. If you have an extra copy of a book you think might add to their collection, make a donation. Remember, it's all tax-deductible.

Oh yes, don't go to your library to use *my* books. Buy them instead. How else can I afford to find the time to write and impart so much good advice?

Why You Should Know About the AASLH

IF you collect, you own a museum. Not many collectors think about their collections in terms of a museum, but that is exactly what the collector has assembled. Further, many of the problems faced by museums are identical to the problems faced by collectors.

The American Association for State and Local History (AASLH), Suite 102, 172 Second Avenue North, Nashville, TN 37201, aids small museums and historical societies, many of which are operated solely by volunteers. AASLH publications provide a wealth of how-to information on managing and caring for a collection, often within the framework of a limited budget. Collectors can obtain a catalog of its publications by writing the AASLH and requesting it.

I own close to fifty AASLH publications and use most of them in the course of year. I want to share with you a few of my favorites. First and foremost is Daniel B. Reibel's *Registration Methods for the Small Museum* ($9.95). This book contains the keys to developing a system to keep track of your collection. The writing style is straightforward and down to earth. It also discusses techniques that are within everyone's pocketbook.

How about caring for your collection? A. Bruce MacLeish is the new author of *The Care of Antiques and Historical Collections* ($14.95). The book was originally written by the late Per E. Guldbeck, a curator at the New York State Historical Association. I had the privilege of studying with Per at two summer institutes held in Cooperstown. His love and concern for the preservation of objects have been a continued source of inspiration to me.

The first eight chapters of the book deal with establishing a complete conservation program for your collection with emphasis on preventive maintenance. Chapters nine through seventeen deal with the care of objects according to category, such as paper, wood, skin and leather, metal, and textiles. Each chapter has an excellent bibliography telling you where to find more detailed information if you need it.

Robert F. McGiffin, Jr., has written *Furniture Care and Conservation* ($18.95),which concentrates on cleaning, repairing, and maintaining historical furniture. McGiffin, an American-trained conservator, translates the technical aspects of conservation into layman's terms.

Everyone has heard of acid-free folders and mats, Hollinger boxes, and other conservation supplies. *Museum Archival Supply Handbook* ($19.95) by the Ontario Museum Association and Toronto Area Archivists Group gives the names of 600 North American suppliers of archival material. Not only is the material described but methods of use are also discussed.

If you are into buying and selling collectibles, museums and historical societies are one of your potential customer sources. How do you locate them? The *Directory of Historical Societies and Agencies*, twelfth edition ($19.95), lists more than 6,000 museums and historical societies. A variety of indexes allows you to pinpoint potential customers in a hurry.

One of the best features of the AASLH is its Technical Leaflet series. More than 140 technical leaflets are available on such diverse subjects as "Care and Display of Glass Collections" (No. 127) to "Tax Problems of the Collector" (No. 31). The leaflets are $2 each. However, the AASLH has prepackaged several series at a greatly reduced cost. I certainly can recommend the fourteen-leaflet "Collections Care" (No. 503 at $7) and the twenty-two leaflet "Collections Management" (No. 504 at $11).

The AASLH also has videotape programs and slide/tape programs. Unfortunately, they cannot be rented and concentrate heavily on interpreting and exhibiting objects rather than on identification and care of specific object categories.

I should write AASLH and ask for a commission on every order that results from my recommendations. I would probably have missed this wonderful source of information had I not begun my career in the museum profession. If you want to preview some of these publications, your local historical society or museum library should have them. Buy the publications that interest you and learn to use them. You'll thank me personally if we ever meet.

Part 6
Sources of Supply

Collectibles at Auction

THE sale of objects in certain collectible categories has become a big business. For example, many early rock'n'roll items, especially those related to Elvis or the Beatles, have broken through the $500 barrier. As a result, most major American auctioneers and auction houses are now actively seeking a share of this rapidly developing market.

Although collectibles are sold at hundreds of auctions each week throughout the United States, my focus here is on those firms that offer a catalog and lists of prices realized.

For the past several years, Sotheby's (1334 York Avenue, New York, NY 10021) has conducted a biannual Collectors' Carrousel auction. The collectibles department is headed by Dana Hawkes and supported by several guest experts. Sotheby's Collectors' Carrousel auctions are strongest in twentieth-century collectibles: animated and comic art, automata and mechanical music, designer fashions, dolls, toys, and rock'n'roll memorabilia.

These auctions focus on big-ticket items, objects that will bring $500 or more per lot. This is the price level at which the firm must sell to meet its catalog and overhead expenses.

In 1985 Sotheby's auctioned the toy collection of Raymond E. Holland, its first attempt at a specialized collectibles auction. The results were mixed, and Sotheby's now includes major collectible collections within its regular Collectors' Carrousel auctions. For example, the June 1988 auction included a major collection of mechanical banks.

Sotheby's London establishment also conducts several auctions a year that focus on twentieth-century collectibles. The record prices for a Beatles object and teddy bear occurred at a London auction. A wise collector makes certain that these catalogs are part of his or her library.

Phillips (406 East 79th Street, New York, NY 10021), whose collectibles department is headed by Henry I. Kurtz, has carved out several key collectible niches in the auction area. Foremost among these is the sale of lead soldiers, especially British. Other categories include animation art, toys, and sports memorabilia.

Recently Phillips was subject to many rumors, ranging from cutting back its New York operation to abandoning the New York scene altogether. Some internal reorganization and refocusing took place to strengthen Phillips's position; the firm will remain in New York. In June 1988 Phillips conducted a collectibles auction of lead soldiers, toys, and sports memorabilia. The quality of the material equaled previous sales.

In the past, Phillips has conducted some specialized collectible sales, most notably an Aeronautica sale several years ago. One hopes that additional specialized sales are in the offing now that Phillips is active again.

The premier American collectibles auction house is Doyle Auctioneers and Appraisers (R.D. 3, Box 137, Fishkill, NY 12524). The decision of Rob and Sue Doyle to focus on collectibles has given the collectibles field the vehicle it needs to test the strength of a wide range of collectible categories.

The firm's catalogs are now in an 8½ by 11" format with most lots illustrated. The Doyles have made a strong effort to improve the quality of the descriptions and to include accurate description reports.

Previously, Doyle Auctioneers and Appraisers conducted specialized sales. Major areas included advertising, gambling and saloon memorabilia, movie memorabilia, musical instruments, and shaving (barber supplies, mugs, razors) items. The catalogs have become the major references for these categories. Doyle Auctioneers and Appraisers now holds only general sales, lumping all categories together. I hope they will not completely abandon the specialized sale.

The Doyles also hold mail auctions. Check their catalogs to see what type of sale is being conducted.

Since the 1970s, specialized auction houses have played a major role in the collectibles auction scene. A leader in this area has been Lloyd Ralston Toys (447 Stratfield Road, Fairfield, CT 06432). Lloyd deserves credit for bringing respectability to and building the toy and toy train auction market. Every lot is illustrated and graded. Ralston's reputation among collectors is excellent.

A new arrival in the toy and game marketplace is Debby and Marty Krim's New England Auction Gallery (Box 2273, West Peabody, MA 01960–7273). The Krims offer a wide range of toys and games, including some as late as the early 1970s. A review of the grading scale indicates that they emphasize items in above-average condition. New England Auction Gallery attracts collectors on a limited budget because its auctions include a number of inexpensive lots.

The Greenbergs (7566 Main Street, Sykesville, MD 21784), whose publications set the standard for the toy train market, now offer a toy-train auction service. Their first auction, held in March 1988, was a resounding success. Further auctions are in the planning stages.

The dominant doll auction firm has been Theriault's (P.O. Box 151, Annapolis, MD 21404). I have spoken with a number of recent consignors who for various reasons seem to be disgruntled. I no longer recommend Theriault's to my friends and clients.

Theriault's is being challenged by Marvin Cohen Auctions (Box 425, New Lebanon, NY 12125). Like Theriault's, Cohen's auctions include dollhouses and doll furniture as well as dolls. Both try to focus on the middle and high end of the doll market spectrum.

Many regional auction houses conduct an occasional auction focusing on a specialized collectible category. In April 1988 Garth's Auctions (P.O. Box 369, Delaware, OH 43015) auctioned a still-bank collection and Noel Barrett Antiques & Auctions Ltd. (Carversville, PA 18912) combined with Richard Opfer Auctioneering, Inc. (Timonium, MD), to sell the George Haney toy collection. The Milwaukee Auction Galleries (318 North Water, Milwaukee, WI 53202) and Mid-Hudson Auction Galleries (One Idlewild Avenue, Cornwall-on-Hudson, NY 12520) also include collectibles in their auctions.

All these firms deserve our thanks for placing the collectible on an equal footing with the antique. I hope they won't rest on these laurels, though, because so many more opportunities are available. The future promises to be exciting.

A Conflict of Interests

ON September 17, 1988, Robert W. Skinner, Inc., sold the games and puzzles of The Game Preserve Museum, the private collection of Lee and Rally Dennis of Peterborough, New Hampshire. The sale was extensively ballyhooed through the trade and daily media, attracting a great deal of attention.

The sale produced some spectacular prices for boxed board games. A Parker Brothers "Toy Town Grocery Store," a miniature grocery diorama, brought $1,800; a Charles B. Darrow "Monopoly" set, $2,400; McLoughlin Brothers "Game of the Visit of Santa Claus," $1,900; McLoughlin Brothers "The Game of the Man in the Moon," $4,600; and McLoughlin Brothers "Game of Baseball," $2,300. The sale firmly established: (1) there are now boxed board games in the $1,000 to $2,500 range; (2) cover lithography influences the price of the game more than any other factor; (3) McLoughlin Brothers material commands a premium; (4) the mystique surrounding the origin of Monopoly drives any pre-Parker Brothers set into the thousands of dollars; and (5) hype fueled by auction fever can drive people mad.

Reports about The Game Preserve Museum sale have focused largely on the high ticket items. Record prices constitute the news. Have we become so fickle that all we want to know any longer about antiques and collectibles is: (a) who bought it and (b) how much was paid for it? An examination of antiques show and auction stories certainly seems to indicate this. To quote Paul Harvey, "It's time for the rest of the story."

I knew The Game Preserve collection well. I photographed it for Lee Dennis's *Warman's Antique American Games, 1840–1940,* first edition (Warman Publishing Company, 1986). Warman has allowed the book to go out-of-print and does not plan to either revise or reprint it. If you own a copy, you own a collectible.

Meanwhile, back at the preserve, the Dennises' collection contained two games with a canal theme, The Chicago Game Company's "Pana Kanal: The Great Panama Canal Game" (1930s) and Milton Bradley's "Through the Locks to the Golden Gate" (ca. 1905), that I very much wanted to add to my own collection. When I heard the news that The Game Preserve Museum was going to be sold, I felt my opportunity was at hand.

I ordered the sale catalog at $14, and eagerly awaited its arrival. When it came, the first thing I noticed was that the sale contained only 315 lots. The Game Preserve Museum contained over a thousand games. My first reaction was that only a portion of the collection was being sold.

Then, reality hit. With a few exceptions that both Skinner and the Dennises expected to bring top dollar, the games and puzzles were not being sold as individual units. Instead, the vast majority were lotted. To get the games that I wanted, I had to buy several that I did not want.

It took me over a half-hour to locate "Through The Locks to the Golden Gate." It was part of Lot 257, "Four Assorted Naval Games," estimated to sell between $250 and $350. I was prepared to pay over $50 for the game, but certainly not $250. The lot actually sold for $125, a sum that still exceeded what I was willing to pay for the game.

I never did find the lot in which the "Pana Kanal" game was included. It must have been in one of the "assorted" lots. Determining which lot required a trip to Bolton, Massachusetts, to attend the preview, a trip that I did not have the time or desire to make.

A sale so heavily lotted is not a sale designed to attract collectors. It is a sale for dealers and interior decorators. The dealers buy the lots cheaply and resell the individual items to specialized collectors at a handsome premium. The decorators snag the pizzazz pieces for clients with unlimited funds and little sense of the true collectible value of the product.

After spending almost an hour with The Game Preserve Museum catalog, I said the heck with it and filed it away. I did not intend to participate in the auction game as it was being dictated.

I was not alone in my frustration. A friend attended the American Game Collectors Association (P. O. Box 1179, Great Neck, NY 11023) annual meeting a week prior to The Game Preserve Museum sale. The AGCA holds an auction as part of its convention festivities. My friend reported: "Auction was a bit dull, though. Everyone was saving up their money for the Game Preserve Auction the following week. I attended and wound up with only one [item]. Most were in lots with several [items], and I didn't want to buy 6 [items] to get 1 [item]."

Knowing Lee and Rally Dennis, I am certain they carefully explored all the alternatives before selling their collection. Any owner wants to sell the collection as a unit, sell it quickly and easily, and achieve the highest return possible. The problem is that these goals often conflict directly with what is best for their fellow collectors.

The ideal approach from a collector's point of view is to sell the items individually. This way, each collector can bid and focus on the pieces that he or she needs. I think this approach was both possible and feasible in respect to The Game Preserve Museum collection.

It was not fair to reduce the collection to only 315 lots. A good auctioneer can sell 60 to 80 lots an hour. Rural auctioneers easily handle 500 and more lots in a day's sale. Day-long sales with 600 to 700 lot counts are not uncommon in the larger New York auction houses. One gets the feeling that Skinner just did not want to be bothered.

The problem with such large auction houses is that high overhead costs force them to seek high-ticket or high-income-producing lots. They think only in terms of $500 and up potential. They simply cannot sell the less expensive material and survive.

Personally, I question the selection of Skinner to handle The Game Preserve Museum sale. Skinner's reputation in the areas of glass, and arts and crafts material is impeccable. In the area of collectibles, it is lightweight. In my opinion, Doyle Auctioneers (R. D. #3, Box 137, Fishkill, NY 12524), New England Auction Gallery (Box 8087, East Lynn, MA 01904), or Lloyd Ralston Toys (447 Stratfield Road, Fairfield, CT 06432) would have done a far better and more sympathetic job representing the Dennises and the collectors. I also think they would have achieved prices just as spectacular as Skinner's.

The material also would easily have lent itself to a mail auction approach. A list of the games with a condition report and minimum bid could have easily been prepared. Lee and Rally did not have to do this. There are any number of mail auction individuals and firms that would have willingly handled the sale.

Currently, the Pearlman Toy Museum in Philadelphia is being sold, using a tag sale system. It is an approach that I think will gain in popularity in the years ahead. While a tag sale would probably not have produced the record-breaking prices that the auction route did for The Game Preserve Museum collection, it would have achieved a far higher return on the middle- and low-end material; thus, I believe, it would have resulted in a higher overall income.

As collectors, we collect because we love the material. We treasure it, yet realize that eventually it will pass to another collector. Collectors do not usually send their material to museums because they want to pass on the joys of ownership to another collector. Collectors ought to carefully consider how to do this in order to achieve maximum distribution among the next generation of collectors. Alas, they do not always do this.

"The Other Doyle"

AMONG my favorite auction houses in America is William Doyle Galleries in New York City. Bill Doyle's operation is the Avis of the business. I don't know anyone who tries harder or is more successful at it than Bill. When someone in the trade says "Doyle's," they generally mean William Doyle Galleries.

But among collectibles collectors, Doyle's does not mean Bill Doyle's New York city operation, but Doyle Auctioneers and Appraisers (R.D. 3, Box 137, Fishkill, New York 12524). For over a decade Rob and Sue Doyle, no relation to Bill Doyle, have suffered under the grossly unfair label of "The Other Doyle." The tremendous effort Rob and Sue have made and the success they have enjoyed in elevating segments of the collectibles field to full catalog status equal to the presentation of the major auction houses for antiques categories are going to make that label obsolete.

Only a few national collectors truly understand the significance of the strong regional auction houses. Recently I tried talking with an employee of a New York auction house about Garth's. She did not even recognize the name. I was afraid to ask her about Roan's or some of the other strong midwest and southern auction houses. What a sheltered world those upscale New York auction devotees live in. The impact of the regional auction houses is growing as they become more and more professional. They now are part of the mainstream of the market. Rob and Sue Doyle are helping lead the movement.

Doyle Auctioneers and Appraisers is a sleeper. No dealer wants to tell his clients about it. Why ruin a good thing—a source of good merchandise at reasonable prices. You may have seen Rob and Sue Doyle's ads in the trade papers, but figured it was too far to travel to Fishkill to attend the sales. You may have been reluctant to take part in their absentee mail auctions because you do not like to bid without seeing the piece. Well, this viewpoint is far too limited.

First, Rob and Sue Doyle's catalogs are among the best in the business, featuring adequate descriptions and condition reports. The detail of their descriptions and condition reports could serve as a model for some of the large New York houses. Most lots are pictured. Rob and Sue Doyle's efforts are almost equal to the catalogs from Ted Hake's Americana & Collectibles, clearly the best in the collectibles field. It is easy to do business with Doyle's via the catalog route.

Second, the staff at Doyle's is friendly and very eager to help. A call evolves quickly into a discussion of the piece in question or a call back when the staff has located the object and has it in front of them.

Third, Doyle's actually does a combination of absentee mail auctions and live auctions, their practice for the past 6½ years. Doyle's uses a 10 percent buyer's premium for live auctions but drops it for the absentee mail auctions. Auctioning collectibles by mail now is an established practice. The key is the reliability of the auction house and its willingness to back the merchandise it sells. On this point, Rob and Sue Doyle are among the leaders in respect to honesty and fairness. Rob encourages bidders who have questions about an object to call before the sale. Hence, his catalogs generally arrive three to four weeks in advance of the auction close.

Fourth, they fairly execute absentee bids. I know some houses that take absentee bids and simply ignore them and others who start pieces at the bid and make the absentee bidder pay the full price. Neither of these factors is a problem at Doyle's.

Fifth, and perhaps most important, within a week of the sale, you have a prices-realized sheet. No price guide can help advanced collectors. They need the results from a good auction house to keep track of the things they collect. Doyle's is among the best I know of in the collectibles category.

A sampling of collectibles categories that have been featured in Doyle's catalog sales since the first of the year include: Shaving Collectibles (advertising, barber items, razors, and shaving mugs), Gambling, Saloon, Advertising, and Old West Collectibles (if it was found in a bar, saloon, or gambling hall, it's here), Movie Memorabilia (equipment, lobby cards, posters, press kits, and more), Posters and Broadsides, Music Material (instruments, music, phonographs), and Americana and Collectibles (you name it).

Several auctions featuring the same themes will reappear later in the year along with auctions on pharmaceutical memorabilia, guns, coins, and small collectibles. Bob and Sue's strength is their willingness to do a single-owner collectible sale provided they can adequately catalog the collection. At this point Doyle's does not do sales of glass and china, unless the object relates to the categories listed above. But who knows? If the right collections comes along, they are ready to try.

Individual catalogs cost $6 each and average between forty and eighty pages. This year Doyle Auctioneers and Appraisers will be conducting fifteen catalog sales. The annual catalog subscription price is $30.

Doyle's has more than 900 subscribers from throughout the United States and foreign countries, including Canada, England, Germany, Switzerland, and Australia. Their computer list of 15,000 collectors allows the targeting of specialized groups, such as the 2,500 individuals that order only the music catalogs.

The high operating costs of doing business in New York city means that houses such as William Doyle Galleries can never afford to concentrate on the collectibles market in the $10 to $500 range. The collectibles collectors will have to look to a regional house to be their major market source. Doyle Auctioneers and Appraiser fits the bill nicely.

Outdoor Fleas

IT is six o'clock in the morning. There is a hint of sun on the horizon; the air is chilly. The dew-dampened grass has completely soaked through shoes and socks. The flashlight batteries are weakening from being turned on and off for the past hour. The coffee consumed an hour earlier is beginning to work, the portable facilities are nowhere in sight – the tire of a truck or a local bush is going to have to do. Over and over again between the hours of six and seven in the morning, the stillness at hundreds of outdoor flea markets throughout the United States is shattered by the flea marketer's lament: "I am having fun; I really am having fun."

The collectors and dealers who attend the nation's outdoor flea markets in the early morning hours are a breed apart. When the annual ten worst-dressed list is published, the first eight or nine positions should be dominated by these flea market regulars. I do not understand why they are not. The early morning disposition of the flea marketer is a cross between a hibernating bear awakened in the middle of February and the cyclops found in the Sindbad movies of late 1950s and early 1960s. Exposing yourself to this treatment is a form of masochism.

Personally, I prefer a more gentle approach. I like to arrive at flea markets after a good night's sleep, eating a hearty breakfast, and watching the morning sun chase away the dew. It just seems to make so much more sense.

I am not concerned about the wealth of bargains that I might have missed by arriving late. The noonday sun and early hours have a profound effect on the dealers. They are pooped; their mental alertness is low. I have negotiated some great deals with flea market dealers in the late afternoon. In addition, I have adequate light in which to inspect the piece. Trying to use a flashlight to inspect an object at a flea market at five in the morning is akin to trying to follow the proverbial bouncing ball. Things simply move too fast; you never focus on something for more than a brief second.

But every auctioneer, collector, dealer, and investor should experience the 5:00 a.m. outdoor flea market ritual at least once in their collecting career. If you really want bragging rights, it has to be an opening day at J & J Promotions (affectionately known in the trade as "The Sisters") field in Brimfield, Massachusetts. The smell of the cooking grease from the outdoor kitchen wafts through the early morning air and gives the term "nauseating" a whole new meaning. I have done it once. That's enough.

A myth has developed that the outdoor flea market is the great wellhead from which goods are disgorged into the market. Bargains abound, waiting only for the eager collector to come scoop them up. The flea market dealers are novices, not really knowing what they have. Alas, this is only a myth.

Today's outdoor flea markets are dominated by a group of professional flea market dealers who travel the circuit. They know their business; they read and use price guides more thoroughly than any other group of dealers. The outdoor flea market is not the home of bargains. Flea markets are as managed and controlled as an antiques show or shop.

But myths die hard. Collectors and others want to believe. As a result, the growth of outdoor flea markets continues. Currently, there appears to be no end in sight.

When you travel outside your home territory, finding flea markets can be a problem. The only national guide is *The Official Directory to U.S. Flea Markets*, second edition (House of Collectibles, 1988), which contains a state-by-state inventory of outdoor and some indoor flea market locations. The list is by no means complete. The introduction superficially covers the methods of buying and selling at flea markets. Anyone wishing to explore the question properly should consult Robert G. Miner's *Flea Market Handbook* (Main Street Books, 1981).

The real key to finding regional and local flea markets is the numerous antiques and collectibles trade newspapers. *The Official Directory to U.S. Flea Markets*, second edition, contains a partial listing. The listing could easily be doubled.

Many trade papers include flea market information in their calendar listings, but the information is often lost among the more numerous auction and show listings. Many also list only their advertisers. As a result, some important local flea markets may not be listed. A few papers group their advertising and list the flea market ads together. This helps. A totally separate flea market section would be even better.

The biggest problem with most flea market advertising is the lack of a map. Many are off the beaten track. The locals know the location, but the out-of-towner needs a course in orienteering to find them. However, I do not want to put all the blame on the trade papers. Flea market operators generally fail to post sufficient directional signs at key highway intersection near their markets.

Anyone who frequents outdoor flea markets knows the quality of the markets varies tremendously. If I could, I would require that every flea market advertisement and/or announcement contain the number of dealers, the hours the market is open to the general public, the admission fee and the time period it covers (one day or the entire length of the flea market), and the time when you can gain early admission by paying the setup fee. A flea market is generally closed to the general public during setup. Experienced collectors and dealers gain early admission to the field by purchasing a space and never setting up.

America is not the only country that is "flea market" crazy. Several flea markets in England and France are over a hundred years old. Even the Germans have caught flea market fever. Recently, I discovered Peter B. Manston's three excellent guides to European flea markets: (1) *Manston's Flea Markets, Antique Fairs, and Auctions of England*, (2) *Manston's Flea Markets, Antique Fairs, and Auctions of France*, and (3) *Manston's Flea Markets, Antique Fairs, and Auctions of Germany*. All are published by Travel Keys, P.O. Box 160691, Sacramento, CA 25816. Their price of $9.95, plus a dollar for shipping and handling, makes them a terrific bargain for the American traveling abroad.

I also like Manston's guides because the introductions contain such useful information as "Getting Your Purchases Home," "Clearing United States Customs," a listing of major auctioneers and auction houses, and clues to finding a toilet. Do not discount the importance of this last piece of information. I would have paid a small fortune for it at 6:00 a.m. on one cold, damp October morning at the Bermondsey Street Antiques Market in London two years ago.

In summary, the outdoor flea market will always be part of the antiques and collectibles scene. However, it is fertile ground only for the experienced veteran, not the neophyte. Outdoor flea markets quickly educate the beginner in the pitfalls of the antiques and collectibles field. Be forewarned. The lessons can be very expensive.

✍

Are Flea Markets Dying?

FROM the early 1960s through the early 1980s, the flea market was one of the most vital sources of buying and selling in the antiques and collectibles field. A major shift is occurring in the late 1980s. The sale of antiques and collectibles through the mail and at hundreds of dealer cooperatives located throughout the United States has replaced the flea market and caused it to enter a period of decline.

Several factors are contributing to this decline. First, many flea markets no longer feature antiques and collectibles alone. I remember my first visit to the Atlanta flea market several years ago. Expecting to find booth after booth of antiques and collectibles, I encountered individuals selling tube socks, plants, seconds and discontinued merchandise, and a wealth of other material that simply can be referred to as junk. When I first attended the great Rose Bowl flea market in Pasadena, California, in the early 1980s, about a third of its space was still devoted to dealers in antiques and collectibles. A visit two years later showed that the space had shrunk to less than ten percent.

Second, the quality of the material at flea markets is steadily deteriorating.

As the editor of *Warman's Antiques and Their Prices* and *Warman's Americana & Collectibles,* I have a good understanding of the major collecting categories that appeal to today's collectors. At a good flea market, eighty to ninety percent of the merchandise should be found in one of the categories in my two books.

In many cases, less than half the merchandise at today's flea markets is listed in my books. The balance is garbage. It does not deserve to be called "antique" or "collectible," let alone be sold in these terms. It belongs in the "used goods" class. In essence, it is nothing more than recycled goods that should be used primarily for utilitarian purposes and then thrown away when they are no longer useful.

The second point is further demonstrated by the large number of objects that are damaged or in very poor condition. The truth is that we are saving a great many things that simply should be thrown out. The fault for this problem rests more with the buyers than with the sellers. We must educate buyers of antiques and collectibles not to buy anything in less than very good condition, unless it is truly rare. If there are no takers for objects in less than very good condition, dealers will quickly get the message and stop offering them for sale.

Third, the flea market circuit has become too crowded. One day flea markets are no longer common. Brimfield is now a week long experience, three times a year. Renninger's Extravaganzas, now expanded to three days each, occur just before the Brimfield flea markets. Dealers do one, then the other. The result is that the buyer who visits both sees the same dealers and the same merchandise over and over and over again.

A professional group of flea market dealers has developed. These dealers operate out of a camper, van, truck, or the back of their car. They are transients, setting up in Florida in the winter and working a gypsy-like circuit through the Midwest, Midatlantic, and New England states the rest of the year. Here this week, five hundred miles away the next week.

Tracking them down becomes a major problem. Recently, a friend in Michigan sent me a note about a Georgia dealer that set up at a Michigan flea market and had some merchandise that I needed for my collection. She was able to obtain his name, address, and phone number for me. Three weeks of phone calls went unanswered. There has been no response to my letter. As I write this column, I still have no idea if he still has the items I would like to buy from him.

Fourth, many flea market dealers have become greedy. The days of unlimited bargains are over. Most flea market dealers are reluctant to put anything out for sale unless they have checked its price in a price guide. Forget what they paid for it; forget the concept of a fair profit and quick return. They want top dollar. They live in the constant fear that something that they sold for ten dollars and for which they paid ten cents will be resold by its purchaser for hundreds, even thousands of dollars.

Traditionally the flea market was the place where merchandise started its trek up the ladder from dealer to dealer and finally to a private collector. A legend grew that an established dealer could attend a flea market, load up a car or truck, return home, and turn a handsome profit from his or her purchases. As collectors found out about the flea markets, they began attending trying to find merchandise at its source.

What ultimately happened is that flea markets, originally the homes for pickers, weekend and part-time dealers, and individuals trying to clean out an accumulation of material from the attic or basement, became nothing more than a place for established dealers in the trade who were simply avoiding the overhead of a shop or booth rent at a show. The flea market is no longer spontaneous; it is permanent.

Fifth, the vast majority of the modern reproductions and fakes that are passed as authentic antiques and collectibles begin the process of falsification in the flea market circuit. The original manufacturers and wholesalers that provide the dealers with the reproductions are properly representing the merchandise at the time of the initial sale. Most of the individuals passing reproductions as originals know what they are doing. They operate through the process of omission. "I do not have any obligation to tell a person the piece is a reproduction unless he specifically asks me if that is the case." Who are they fooling? Many of us, I fear.

Every collector and dealer has encountered some great finds at flea markets. I am no exception. The memories of these tend to linger far longer than the memories of the failures. Rarely do we count the time we spent looking, the cost for gas, food, and lodging, and the decay to clothing caused by dust and mud.

In many cases, the word "flea market" in today's vocabulary is a misnomer. Renningers, in Adamstown, Pennsylvania, is no longer a true flea market. It is a place where dealers rent and maintain a permanent booth. Merchandise is stored in the booth from week to week. Many flea markets such as Renningers are really dealer consortiums in disguise.

The traditional outdoor flea market circuit is not going to vanish. It will always be with us. But, no phase of the antiques and collectibles business reigns as "top dog" forever. Times change. During one period the auction house may be dominant, during another the shop owner. The flea market has enjoyed its period of dominance. It is time for a new "top dog."

Part 7
Collectible Categories

Animal Collectors

I have often written about Rinker's Thirty-Year Rule: "For the first thirty years in anything's life, all its value is speculative." It helps put the purchase of limited-edition material and contemporary collectible crazes, such as Star Trek, into perspective. Rinker's Thirty-Year Rule allows time for the vast majority of objects to be discarded or deteriorate, sufficient buying and selling to take place to establish a steady market, and collectors to become rich enough to buy back their childhood. There are exceptions to most general rules. Rinker's Thirty-Year Rule is no exception.

Animal collectors, those individuals who collect a specific animal theme—cat, cow, dog, frog, horse, pig—provide the principal exception to my rule. These collectors rarely care if the item was made yesterday or three hundred years ago. Age is not a critical factor. As long as the object is in the shape of their favorite animal or has their favorite animal pictured on it, they want it.

The love of the animal motivates the animal collector, not the object. As a result of their almost fanatical devotion to the animal theme, animal collectors often do not discriminate in respect to the quality of the objects they collect. Aesthetically pleasing or just plain junk, it makes no difference. Cuteness often counts more than aesthetic quality. This nonchalant attitude of the animal collector drives the sophisticated collector mad.

The animal collector also gives meaning to the phrase: "There is never enough." The animal collector wants it all, every possible example. There is only one way that animal collectors measure whether or not they have a good collection—size. They think in terms of hundreds, some even in terms of thousands. Why not? This quantity of material exists. Finding it is not that difficult.

Animal collectors' biggest problem is finding enough money to buy all the collectibles that they find. There are more buying opportunities than money available. Because the emphasis is on size of collection, animal collectors often will not pay a high price for a single object. The animal collector will resolve to do without and look for something else.

Animal collectors are cross-category collectors. Almost every collectible category offers the potential of finding an object with a favorite animal portrayed on it. A Rin-Tin-Tin lunch box will be coveted not only by the dog and German Shepherd collectors but also by the character, cowboy, movie, and television collectors. Reality indicates that the latter group usually will pay far more for the piece than will the animal collectors.

This is especially true if the animal portrayal is in the background. The animal collector wants the animal front and foremost. They do not think of their favorite animal as secondary; and, I suspect, they secretly resent anyone who does.

The collector also wants the animal to be identifiable. The vast majority of animal collectors are not big on abstract representations. They also want the animal positively portrayed. They do not have the ability to laugh at humor that puts their favorite animal in a precarious or torturous position. Attack their animal, you attack them. Objectivity is not an issue; everything written or spoken about their favorite animal is taken personally.

Novice animal collectors tend to concentrate their collection in one specific location. I once visited a person who was a frog collector. She kept her collection in the guest bathroom. From floor to ceiling the green frog motif was everywhere. The toilet was green, the toilet paper featured frogs, the soap was in the shape of a frog, the wastebasket was a frog. You get the picture.

Serious collectors scatter their animals throughout their home and office and often wear clothing and accessories that accent their love for their favorite animal. You never have any trouble identifying where their interest lies. Do not ask a question about their collection unless you are prepared to stay for hours. They want and need to share their enthusiasm with others.

Of all the collectible collectors, animal collectors are among the best organized. The following list of collectors' clubs illustrates this point:

American Association of Aardvark Afficionadoes, 7 Russel Place, Summit, NJ 07901

Cat Collectors, 31311 Blair Drive, Warren, MI 48092

The Canine Collector's Companion, P.O. Box 2948, Portland, OR 97208

The National Elephant Collector's Society, 380 Medford Street, Somerville, MA 02145

The Frog Pond, P.O. Box 193, Beech Grove, IN 46107

Horsin' Around, Box 4764, New River Ridge II, Phoenix, AZ 85207

Russell's Owl Collector's Club, P.O. Box 1292, Bandon, OR 97411

Unicorns Unanimous, 248 North Larchmont Building, Los Angeles, CA 90004

Wee Scots, Inc., National Scottie Dog Collectors Club, P.O. Box 1512, Columbus, IN 47202

I would be remiss if I did not mention the International Society of Animal License Collectors (4420 Wisconsin Avenue, Tampa, FL 33616). Although concentrating heavily on dog licenses, the society also features information about camel, goat, monkey, mule, skunk, turtle, and wolf licenses as well. Animal-license collectors make a strong distinction between licenses and rabies vaccination tags. Rabies tags are not eagerly sought by collectors at this time.

I enjoy writing and talking with animal collectors. Marilyn Dipboye, a cat collector, always signs her letters, "purringly yours." It makes a statement, doesn't it? I understand the president of the frog collectors is called the chief croaker. I will let you decide what type of statement this makes.

Do not assume that the absence of a collectors' club means that the animal category is not collectible. *Au contraire.* The trade papers are filled with individuals looking for cow, elk, flamingo, moose, penguin, and pig items. A simple basic assumption is that every animal theme is collectible.

Occasionally, a collector will specialize and focus only on one breed of animal. This is especially true for dog collectors. These specialized collections often contain a higher quality of objects because the collector is willing to pay more to get an example dealing with a specific, favored breed. With this exception, however, all the points raised above still apply.

The animal collector is indeed a breed apart from the average collectibles collector. How do I know? My wife collects cats.

Is My Autograph Authentic?

MY mother's Uncle Tom remained a bachelor all his life. One of his proudest possessions was a personalized, autographed glossy photograph of Jean Harlow. If he only had known he had been schnookered by Jean's mother, who actually signed the photograph, I suspect his opinion of the famous actress would have changed considerably. Fortunately Uncle Tom died before I learned enough to shatter his dreams.

Recently I talked with Cordelia and Tom Platt, autograph dealers located at 2806 Church Road, Cherry Hill, NJ 08002. Cordelia and Tom have prepared a sheet of guidelines for beginning collectors of autographed material (send a self-addressed stamped envelope). One topic on the sheet deals with the authenticity of autographs.

I am amazed at the number of people who think all signatures are authentic.

Imagine how many requests for signatures individuals such as President Reagan, Elizabeth Taylor, Pete Rose, or Don Johnson receive. They simply do not have the time to sit down and sign everything that bears their signature.

More often than not, signatures are ghost written—a secretary, friend, or relative signs the material for the person. Presidents Nixon and Kennedy are famous for the secretaries who signed their memos, general correspondence, and photographs. The practice was especially prevalent in the entertainment field in the 1920s and 1930s.

The biggest problem for today's autograph collectors is the autopen, a device that does up to 300 signatures in an hour. A facsimile signature is inscribed in a plate that serves as the template for the mechanically driven pen. However, the autopen is not new. It has been used for several decades by famous individuals, especially politicians.

Another problem is represented by the imprinted or lithographed signature. One method involves placing a signature on an item, photographing it, and running off the finished product by the thousands. A second method is printing directly on the photograph or document, often in an ink that contrasts with the background of the item.

Rudolph Valentino was famous for using a wide variety of metal stamps to "sign" his photographs. Other famous personalities had rubber stamps made of their signature for agents, secretaries, and others to use.

Of course, there are many outright forgeries. I have in my collection a signed photograph by John F. Kennedy and Charles de Gaulle. When you remove the mounting paper attached to the back, the photograph has the stamp of the Kennedy Library. The print obviously was issued after Kennedy's death and therefore cannot contain a real signature.

How do you know if you have the real thing? First, ask yourself if it is logical to assume that the individual would actually sign this type of document. Movie stars do not carry around glossy photographs with them.

Second, examine the signature closely. By all means use a magnifying glass. You should be able to spot a printed signature quickly by this method.

Third, look at the signature itself. If the strokes in the signature are extremely consistent, if the signature does not show an impression from the pressure of writing or is uniform in ink flow (a true signature will be light in some areas and darker in others), then an alarm signal should go off.

Fourth, consult the books containing facsimile signatures. Charles Hamilton's *American Autographs* (Norman, OK: University of Oklahoma Press, 1983) is excellent for the signers of the Declaration of Independence, Revolutionary War leaders, and presidents, albeit rather expensive. Hamilton's *Collecting Autographs and Manuscripts* is much more helpful but now out of print. Grab a copy for your library when you see one. The new autograph collectors' bible is George Sanders, Helen Sanders, and Ralph Roberts' *The Price Guide to Autographs* (Wallace-Homestead: 1988); which contains not only a wealth of facsimile signatures but also a comprehensive listing of prices, detailed answers to the basic questions about autograph collecting, and a list of autograph dealers and their addresses.

Because of my work and travels, I frequently encounter famous personalities from all walks of life. Whenever I obtain their signature, I also type up a brief note to file with it indicating the date and location where the signature was obtained. This goes a long way in authenticating the signature because the owner can check to make certain both the person in question and I were in that location on that date.

"Off We Go into the Wild Blue Yonder . . ."

THE last time that you traveled aboard an airplane, did you leave the plane with anything besides your luggage and carry-on baggage? If not, stop here and do not read further. I do not want to give you heartburn. If you did, you are truly a collector with vision.

An airplane is ripe with collectibles, from dinnerware and glasses, eating utensils, junior pilot wings, magazines, menus, motion-discomfort bags (barf bags), playing cards, postcards, and time schedules to safety cards, "seat occupied" cards, and swizzle sticks. In fact, anything with an airline's logo has potential value to airline collectors.

The terminal provides another opportunity to obtain airline collectibles. Time schedules are the most obvious. Baggage-destination stickers, baggage labels, special promotion material, and assorted other giveaways are usually available. A surprising amount of the material is free for the taking.

Make friends with the employees behind the ticket counters. Ask them to save you signs and other advertising material when it becomes obsolete. They are an excellent source for airline company letterhead and other paper products from the operation sector. Another good source for this type of material is your travel agent.

What about famous aviators and pilots? Items associated with Richard E. Bird, Douglas Corrigan, Glenn Curtiss, Amelia Earhart, Charles Lindbergh, Eddie Rickenbacker, and the Wright Brothers are eagerly sought by airline collectors. A "Welcome Corrigan" ribbon and badge from his August 8, 1938, appearance in Boston books at $40. Amelia Earhart's autograph on a white card fetches $175 or more. A pair of bronze-washed iron Charles Lindbergh bookends sells for over $60.

In the 1950s flying 100,000 miles on a commercial airline was considered a major accomplishment. Many airlines gave handsome wooden plaques with an engraved metal nameplate to individuals who passed this milestone. They are eagerly sought by collectors. Today airlines use frequent-flyer plans as incentives. Participation usually results in receiving a plastic membership card, similar in size to a credit card. It does not cost you anything to join, so join as many as you can. Remember, plastic lasts forever.

Do not forget airline personnel. Their uniforms and insignia are collectible. I am not suggesting that you attack and strip them in public or private. But if you have a friend who works or had worked for an airline, ask to buy their obsolete uniforms, employees badges, and manuals.

Within the past decade, a number of airlines have merged or gone out of business. While Piedmont was becoming part of USAir, smart collectors were stashing away collectible Piedmont material. I have found from past experience that when a merger or acquisition occurs, the new company has only one desire — to get rid of everything with the old name on it as quickly as possible. You will be too late if you wait until the change occurs. The garbage man will get the material instead of you.

People's and Braniff are gone completely. If one goes back to the beginning of commercial aviation, a list of airlines no longer operating would fill pages. Material from these airlines commands a premium.

Finally, there are the components or the plane itself. David Lindquist, owner of the Whitehall Shop in Chapel Hill, North Carolina, sold a World War I pilot's seat for over $1,000. The recent flap over the maintenance level of Continental and Eastern planes revealed that commercial airliners have a limited lifetime. What happens to all those goodies that are stripped from an airline when it is readied for resale to someone else? Time to check out the maintenance and refitting hangars at your major airports.

Warman's Americana & Collectibles, third edition (Warman Publishing Company, 1987), contains a section on aeronautica, another name for airline memorabilia. There are also several books devoted exclusively to aspects of airline collectibles. Stan Baumwald (2430 NE 35th Street, Lighthouse Point, FL 33064) publishes *Junior Crew Member Wings*, a detailed catalog listing of all junior crew member wings located to date. Stan updates the book every June. Fred Chan (P.O. Box 473, Burtonsville, MD 20866) and Trev Davis (Essendon, Australia) compiled *Airline Playing Cards: An Illustrated Reference Guide*, now in its second edition. The cooperation between these two authors illustrates the worldwide appeal of airline memorabilia. Finally, the Aeronautica & Air Label Collectors Club—Aerophilatelic Federation of America has published *Air Transport Label Catalog*.

Collectors of airline memorabilia are organized. The World Airline Historical Society is located at 3381 Apple Tree Lane, Erlanger, KY 41018. The society issues the *Captain's Log*, a quarterly journal. In addition to focusing on collectibles, the society also covers model making and the study of the history of airlines and airliners. A complete membership roster is published at the beginning of each year. The current annual membership fee is $14.

The society has regional chapters. Each year one or more of the clubs hosts the annual convention. The announcement of the society's 1988 convention in Denver included information that there would be "200 display/trade/sell tables (that) will provide lots of memorabilia for all and probably a diminishing of your wallet as well." They cannot be faulted for their honesty.

Here I have chosen to focus on civilian airlines. But do not forget the United States Air Force and its memorabilia. Every point I made about civilian airline memorabilia goes double for Air Force material. Most collectors of Air Force material belong to one or more of the militaria collectors' groups.

There is one additional group about which you should be aware: The F-4 Phantom Society (3381 Apple Tree Lane, Erlanger, KY 41018). The society is open to any individual or group interested in the study and preservation of the McDonnell Douglas F-4 Phantom II jet. The society issues *Smoke Trails*, a quarterly publication.

Well, the next time that you are up in the wild blue yonder with time to kill, you now know what to do. Roam around and pick up a few airline collectibles. Just make certain the captain has turned off the seat-belt sign.

Take Me out to the Ball Game

IT'S not reality for an old baseball player to die with his gloves and spikes on. The mementos of his playing days usually have been relegated to the trash, the closet, a collector's den, or the Baseball Hall of Fame long before his death. However, old baseball players do not "fade away" in the tradition of the old soldier so aptly recalled by General MacArthur.

What happens to old baseball players? Many show up at baseball card and memorabilia or collectibles shows signing autographs. Their appearance often is an event rivaling the best of the Roman circuses.

Have you ever attended a baseball card and memorabilia show? Baseball card and memorabilia collectors are a breed apart from the "normal" collectors. They prefer to associate only with their own kind. As a result, they have their own show circuit independent of the traditional antiques and collectibles show circuit. The same is true for the doll, firearms, toy, and train collectors. But these groups are not as organized and fanatical as the baseball collectors.

I attended a baseball show a few years ago at a large suburban motel. I waited in line for over an hour to get into the show. The room became so crowded that the fire marshall refused to allow anyone else to enter until someone left. Wouldn't most antiques and collectibles show promoters love to have this problem?

Joe DiMaggio, the Yankee Clipper, was in attendance at the show signing autographs. You paid five dollars extra for Joe's autograph. Furthermore, you had to supply the item to be autographed, and Joe would only sign his name. It was explained that if Joe had to personalize the material, he would collapse with exhaustion before the day was complete.

What does all this mean to the youngster who stood patiently by the tunnel, the door to the dressing room, or the exit to the stadium to glimpse his hero and obtain his signature? Is a signature from the playing days of a baseball great worth the same as a modern signature issued twenty to forty years later? Alas, both signatures are valued about the same. It does not seem right, but it is.

Recently I was asked by Shirley Swaab, a good friend and organizer of the antiques and collectibles lecture program for Cheltenham Township (Pennsylvania) Adult School, to prepare a lecture entitled "Weird and Strange Things People Collect." The baseball field provided one of the weirdest—cracked baseball bats.

I never laid awake nights wondering what happened to all those game-used (substitute the word, "broken") bats that resulted from game after game. Well, Bill Colby (Kenrich Company, 9418-S Las Tunas Drive, Temple City, CA 91780) did. Where others saw only broken pieces, he saw gold. Bill began buying game-used bats through club property men and batboys. Collectors bought them eagerly. Selling broken baseball bats and other sports memorabilia has become a full-time business with Bill.

How do you rationalize owning a broken baseball bat? Well, if you want a Pete Rose bat for your collection, you can write to Hillerich & Bradsby, the makers of Louisville Slugger, and order one. But Pete Rose will never have touched your bat, making it less valuable in the eyes of most baseball collectors. Buying a game-used, broken bat with Pete Rose's name on it almost ensures that it is a bat that Pete actually used. We are not talking peanuts and crackerjack here. We are talking big bucks. Game-used bats by superstars like Pete Rose and Mike Schmidt can sell for up to $150. Broken bats in the $50 range include stars such as Pedro Guerrero, Kent Hrbek, Bill Madlock, and Dave Parker. An average player's bat brings $8 to $12.

So much for active players. Suppose you get lucky enough to own a game-used bat by one of the superstars from the past. The following prices are listed in Don Raycraft and Stew Salowitz's *Collector's Guide to Baseball Memorabilia* (Collector Books, 1986): Ty Cobb at $1,500 to $2,000, Honus Wagner at $1,100 to $1,500, Babe Ruth at $850 to $1,200 (Babe apparently handed out too many of his bats), and Paul Waner at $300 to $450.

The modern baseball collector wants anything associated with the sport and worn by a player. This includes hats, batting helmets, uniforms, batting gloves, socks, and shoes. If I was Pete Rose or Mike Schmidt, I would be sewing nametags on my underwear. There is money to be made. They are well advised not to miss the opportunity.

Finally, I am glad to see the baseball enthusiasts expanding their horizons beyond the baseball card. I have felt for a long time that the heavy emphasis put on baseball cards has overshadowed some of the more exciting baseball collectibles, from equipment to programs and baseball park souvenirs to items from other collectible groups using a baseball theme. As I was working with Lee Dennis on *Warman's Antique American Games, 1840–1940* (Warman Publishing Company, 1986), I was fascinated by how many games had a baseball theme, ranging from Milton Bradley's "Babe" Ruth's Baseball Game valued at $175 to Toy Creations's Official Radio Baseball Game at $40. In fact, the first antique game to break the $1,000 barrier had a baseball theme.

Collecting baseball memorabilia, especially from the 1960s and later, remains fairly inexpensive. There is an aspect of baseball memorabilia to fit everyone's pocket. Of all our collecting fields, it is the one that is turning on the largest number of young people. There are opportunities for us oldtimers as well. Let's show those youngsters we haven't forgotten how to "play ball."

[Note: On September 17, 1988, Robert W. Skinner, Inc., sold The Game Preserve Museum Collection, the collection assembled by Lee and Rally Dennis. At that

auction, Milton Bradley's Babe Ruth Baseball Game realized $770, Philadelphia Game Mfg. Co.'s Major League Baseball Game $715, McLouglin Bros.' Game of Base-Ball $2,530, and Crebnelle Novelty Company's Championship Baseball Parlor Game $1,430.]

I Have a Set of China . . .

EACH week I receive at least one letter from an individual who has inherited her grandmother's or mother's set of china, for which she wants to find replacement pieces or learn its value. If I answered these letters individually, I would be repeating the same information over and over again. What follows will resolve ninety-five percent or more of this type of inquiry.

How many people do you know who collect china services? I am not aware of any. The result is that while grandmother's and mother's china service may be old, it has minimal antique value unless it dates prior to 1840 or was owned by some famous person. Its value rests solely with finding an individual who wants to purchase it for personal use. No buyer, no value—it is that simple.

Individuals buy old china services for many reasons. First and foremost is that many old services have a wealth of serving pieces that simply are not available in today's patterns. A modern service might feature three sizes of serving platters; an older service might have six or more sizes. If your old china service does not have a large number of serving pieces, its value to a potential buyer is minimized.

A second reason for buying an old china service is to acquire a distinctive pattern, one that is not identical to that of your neighbor or best friend. The number of china patterns in today's market is small compared to the large number of patterns that were available between 1880 and 1920. Haviland alone produced more than 66,000 china service patterns in this 40 year period.

When evaluating an old china service, the adage that "beauty is in the eye of the beholder" applies. The pattern of the service you have may appear perfectly lovely to you; but there is no guarantee that someone else may feel the same way. My own experience indicates that for old china the airy, pastel floral patterns sell best, followed by ornate Victorian patterns. Highly unusual patterns are often difficult to sell. People use china services when entertaining. Guests compliment patterns that they easily recognize. They may not respond favorably to a nontraditional pattern.

Do the research necessary to identify the maker, pattern, and date of your china service. Limoges is not a manufacturer; it is a town in France. There were and still are many pottery and porcelain manufacturers in Limoges, not the least of which is Haviland.

Reference books are available. A welcome recent addition is Susan and Al Bagdade's *Warman's English & Continental Pottery & Porcelain: An Illustrated Price Guide* (Warman Publishing Company, 1987). The book contains information on more than two hundred of the major European manufacturers, including references to specialized books about the companies. You can locate reference books to American manufacturers by checking the appropriate categories in *Warman's Antiques and Their Prices* and *Warman's Americana & Collectibles.*

Before World War I Americans exhibited a strong preference for English- and Continental-made china services. Many American manufacturers' marks and pattern names had a distinct English appearance. After 1920 Japanese and American china services made major inroads into the market. Today, a service of Homer Laughlin's Fiesta ware or Noritake azalea pattern china commands the same price as many turn-of-the-century Haviland patterns.

Most modern buyers of an old china service no longer make the manufacturer a primary consideration in their selection. Few dinner guests turn over a dinner plate to check the maker. I'm an exception; I like to know if my hosts are using their best china for my visit. Our modern buyer is concerned first about the pattern, second the number of place settings and serving pieces, third condition, and finally the availability of replacement pieces.

Within the past ten years, a number of antiques and collectibles dealers have specialized in providing matching services for china and glass patterns. Many advertise regularly in the trade papers. Ralph and Terry Kovel's *The Kovel's Collectors' Source Book* (Crown Publishers, 1983) has a chapter entitled "Matching Services," which identifies more than fifty china dealers and their specialties. Most matching services keep detailed records of their customers' wants and eagerly search out china to satisfy them.

Matching-service dealers have hundreds of sets of china on hand. The dealer usually must buy an entire set for inventory. But his customers often want only one or two pieces, such as a cup to replace one that was broken or a special serving piece. For this reason, the individual cost per piece is high. What one pays a matching service for a single piece is no barometer for judging the worth of a complete set. In order to survive, the matching-service dealer must recover what he paid for the service and make a fair profit from the sale of the first few pieces. He has no way of knowing how long the odd pieces will remain in inventory.

A china service might be worth more broken up, especially if it has a large number of serving pieces, than if it is kept together as a set. Individuals are willing to use unmatched serving pieces, especially if the pattern is close to theirs. I have seen serving pieces of Royal Worcester and Haviland sold individually at five to ten times what they would bring if kept in the service.

Many china services fall into a relatively small number of price levels. An English or Continental porcelain china service with eight place settings and fifteen to twenty service pieces from 1880 to 1920 is in the $1,000 to $1,500 range. Increasing the place settings to twelve and the serving pieces to twenty-plus jumps the price to $1,500 to $2,000. Add another twenty to fifty percent for bone china. A mid-twentieth century American or Japanese porcelain china service for eight with ten to fifteen service pieces sells for $500 to $600. Additional place settings and key serving pieces add about $50 more per unit.

A developing trend in the market is the collectibility of American-manufactured glazed pottery and china dinner services of the 1920s through the 1940s. Jo Cunningham's *The Collectors' Encyclopedia of American Dinnerware* (Collector Books, 1982) and Betty Newbound's *The Gunshot Guide to Values of American Made China and Pottery, Book 2* (privately printed, 1983) are the basic price guides. Specialized price guides exist for Blue Ridge, Coors, Franciscan Ware, Monmouth-Western Stoneware, and Purinton Pottery. *The Daze* (Box 57, Otisville, MI 48463) is the leading vehicle through which American dinnerware is bought and sold.

In summary, have you become rich as a result of inheriting your grandmother's or mother's china service? The answer is no. Are you going to be happy if you ever contemplate selling the service? Unless you are easily satisfied, the chances are again that the answer will be no. First, the service has a great deal of nostalgic value. You will never get what you think it ought to be worth. Second, you will go to a jewelry or department store, note the high cost of present-day china services, and conclude that your old service should certainly be worth more than these modern things. Alas, this is not the case.

What should you do? Use it! Enjoy it! Find a matching service that can provide extra pieces if you break one. However, wash it by hand. Most of the old china services were not designed for the high temperature of dishwasher water. Finally, if all else fails, do what your grandmother and mother did. Give it to your children and let it be their problem.

✍

"Mildly Microwaved, Pre-Pubescent, Kung-Fu Gophers"

WHEN was the last time you shopped for comic books? Because Harry Jr., my son, is a comic book devotee, and his daily activities prevent him from visiting the comic emporiums near Fort Lewis, Washington, where he is a student in the Khaki College, he relies on good old dad to make a monthly trip to Beachead Comics in Allentown to pick up the issues he needs to maintain his runs of the "Fantastic Four," " Cloak and Dagger," " Droids," and titles of similar ilk.

Personally, I think this onerous duty falls under the little-understood concept of parental abuse, practiced with some skill by the current generation of "what can you do for me" children. Harry Jr. has a master's degree in this discipline without ever having attended college.

Of course, I have to shoulder some of the blame in this instance since I continually stressed to Harry Jr. that things should be acquired and kept in as near mint condition as possible. I told him comic books should not be ordered through the mail, where damage in shipment is almost guaranteed, but secured at the local comic book shop, where one can carefully inspect covers and contents before purchasing.

During a recent visit to Beachead Comics, I glanced at a shelf and saw the No. 1 issue of "Mildly Microwaved, Pre-Pubescent, Kung-Fu Gophers." This thirty-two-page comic with only a black-and-white interior is published by Just Imagine Graphix, Ltd., and sells for a mind-boggling $1.50. I bought one!

A conversation with the owner of Beachead revealed that the hottest comics of the moment are mutant animal topics. Among the available titles are "Pre-Teen, Dirty-Gene, Kung-Fu Kangaroos," "Boris the Bear," who fortunately slaughtered the teenager, radioactive, blackbelt, mutant, ninja critters in a recent issue, and "Grown-Up Thermonuclear Samurai Elephants."

In 1954, right in the middle of my most formative period, Fredric Wertham wrote *Seduction of the Innocent,* a scathing attack on comics. Wertham pointed a guilt-laden finger at the comic industry for corrupting youth, causing juvenile delinquency, and undermining American values. Parents across the nation confiscated such fantasy epics as "Frontline Combat," "The Human Torch," "Crime Smashers," "Roy Rogers," "Donald Duck," or "Confessions of Love."

Seduction of the Innocent forced many publishers out of the comic business. Is there an analogy to the modern critics of record lyrics or the reputed decadence of MTV? Some publishers established a "comics code" to assure parents that their comics were compliant with morality and decency standards developed by the code authority.

Heck, when you are thirteen, morality and decency don't look as formidable as they do when you get older. All I wanted was my weekly comic fix; for, in reality, I was one of the comic book junkies about which Wertham was so concerned.

The supplier of my addiction was my mother, who managed the newspaper and magazine section of Prosser's Drug Store in Hellertown, Pennsylvania. As the new comic books arrived, my mother brought them home for me to do a quick read before she put them on the newstand for sale. I had a fifty-book-a-week habit.

Now don't get me wrong. Anyone who knew my mother will attest to the fact that she also acted as the moral censor for all literature sold at Prosser's. Only Uncle Bill and a select few had access to the girlie magazines in the drawer in the back room. They were never sold over the counter.

Mother made certain that I did not get to read the horror comics, science fiction, or romance comics. The lack of exposure to the latter group is no doubt responsible for my suppressed romantic libido since I was not able to study the "how-to" lessons.

Instead, I learned to speed read, keep over a hundred storylines alive in my mind at one time, and handle objects carefully (remember, the comics had to look like they had not been read). If you stop and think about it, these are skills I use everyday.

I cannot think of my high school contemporaries without thinking of comics. I would be willing to bet that over half the book reports submitted to teachers at Hellertown High School during the 1950s were done from Classic Comics.

There was an innocence attached to a generation of teenagers who followed the adventures of Archie, Betty, and Veronica almost as religiously as they did Elvis.

I guess the one thing I owe to comic books more than anything else is that it kept alive my ability to dream and fantasize. In a way, I also think it taught me the acceptable limits to these pursuits. I suppose this is why I never cracked down on how much time Harry Jr. spent playing Dungeons and Dragons. Better he should escape from reality in this fashion than with drugs.

Perhaps I owe Harry Jr. a degree of thanks for reintroducing me to the world of comics. I recently renewed acquaintances with a number of old friends, from Batman to Wonder Woman. I must admit I am having a little trouble with the new image of The Man of Steel, but I bought the first six issues nevertheless.

Somehow I don't think I will ever be comfortable with the "New Mutants," "Alien Ducklings," or "Hamster Vice." But knowing me, I'll buy a few issues just to have them around.

Who knows, in fifty years, when a museum is doing a major exhibit on the comics of the 1980s, my heirs may have the only copy available for display of "Mildly Microwaved, Pre-Pubescent, Kung-Fu Gophers."

Excuse Me While I Powder My Nose

WHEN I see a compact, I think of 1940s and 1950s mystery movies. An actress, possibly Betty Grable, Rita Hayworth, or Lana Turner, is being pursued. She seeks refuge in a restaurant or a crowded room at a sporting event or hotel. She is nervous. Where is her pursuer? She reaches in her purse, pulls out her compact, and uses the mirror to scan the room. The pursuer's image appears in her compact mirror. The suspense is enormous. A quick dash out the back door or into the ladies room to escape by the window averts disaster.

The use of makeup became fashionable in the last quarter of the nineteenth century. The natural look, achieved through proper diet and exercise, was replaced by substances designed to give women a "beautiful healthy tint." As women began applying rouge, powdering their noses, coating their lips, and enhancing their eyes with shadow and mascara, they wanted to make certain that these important substances so necessary in maintaining a femme fatale look were readily available. Manufacturers responded.

Initially makeup was carried in vanity bags or cases. I'll let you guess why the name never stuck. By the 1930s and 1940s the word "compact" became the accepted nomenclature.

I grew up during the "golden" era of compacts, the 1940s and 1950s. I never remember my mother without one. I remember how frustrated I used to get when my dinner date went into the ladies room to "freshen up" or "powder her nose." I always felt bathrooms were designed for an entirely different function.

The basic compact held powder and had a mirror in the lid. More elaborate examples contained compartments for cake rouge, lipstick, cigarettes, and even a dime. The latter was a safety value for a quick call home in case of emergency.

Although the compact was essentially functional, it came in an infinite variety of designs. It is this diversity that has begun to attract collectors. Just as with jewelry and other decorative accessories, compacts frequently incorporated the most advanced stylistic elements of their period. It is possible to view many of the sophisticated examples as works of art.

Art Deco compacts fascinate me more than any others. The geometric designs in bold colors, often done in enamel, are a treat to the eye. Prices range from $45 to $150 for examples in the middle price range. However, style is just one collecting criteria.

Compacts often served as advertising giveaways, souvenirs, or remembrances of a special event. Cigarette companies gave away compacts that contained makeup as well as a compartment for their product. Travelers aboard the 1939 voyages of the RMS *Mauretania* could purchase an oval compact with a picture of the ship on the cover. Three different "Scarlett O'Hara" compacts accompanied the release of the film "Gone With the Wind" in 1940. One collector owns an example awarded as the first-place prize for Rainbow Room dancing contests in the 1930s and 1940s. The front contains a photograph of Tony and Sally Demarco dancing.

Novelty compacts offer a challenging collecting approach. In 1910 the hatpin industry introduced ornamental hatpins with heads large enough to hold powder puffs, mirrors, trinkets, or small change. The heads often contained imitation gemstones or incised designs. Canes, bracelets, and purses are just three more examples of objects that had compacts built into them.

Although most compact collectors seem to have broad-reaching collections, specialized collectors have developed. One collector concentrates on compacts with a Scottie dog theme in shape or design; another seeks compacts with pictures of Charlie McCarthy.

Compact collecting is in its early stages. Previously compact collections were assembled as secondary aspects of some other specialized collection. The key to viewing the compact as a separate collecting entity can be traced to the "natural" look that dominated the 1960s and 1970s and caused compacts to virtually disappear. The pre-1960 examples became classic or vintage pieces.

The vast majority of vintage compacts still sell between $10 and $100. The cost and the fact that you can store a large number in a small space make them ideal for the young, urban collector. Among the things that can drive the cost of a compact through the $100 barrier are highly stylistic designs, use of precious stones or gold on the cover, and handcrafted examples by famous artists and designers.

In 1987 several collectors formed The Compact Collectors Club (P.O. Box S, Lynbrook, NY 11563) with annual dues of $15. The club's quarterly newsletter, *Powder Puff*, contains articles concerning the history, preservation, display, and valuing of vintage compacts, personal collecting experiences of members, and a "seekers, sellers, and swappers" column.

The Winter 1988 issue of *Powder Puff* chronicles the arrival of a new generation of compacts. Yves Saint Laurent offers a heart-shaped compact for $75; Clinique has a silver-plated compact for $37. Stratton of London makes a variety of compacts priced between $22 and $80. Even Estée Lauder has joined the bandwagon.

Roselyn Gerson, *Powder Puff's* editor, questions whether these new examples can capture "the intricate and exacting workmanship on some of our collectibles compacts." I've heard that song plenty of times before from established collectors. I plan to stash away some of the more stylistic modern examples. Collectors in 2038 will be glad I did.

The publication of Roselyn Gerson's *Vintage Ladies' Compacts* (Wallace-Homestead: 1989) marks the coming of age of compact collecting. Over 2,000 compacts are priced and illustrated. The book has the potential to be a trigger that will send the prices for compacts soaring in the years ahead.

Are we about to enter an era when the term "pancake" will again have a double meaning? One look at Tammy Bakker, and the answer is obvious.

Those Old Diplomas

WHERE is your high school or college diploma? How about your confirmation certificate? Do you care?

Recently Jocelyn Butterer, a former assistant editor at Warman's, was attending an auction in eastern Pennsylvania. Near the end of the sale a box lot was offered that contained three framed documents, one a diploma, bearing the name Roland J. Wotring. Since Jocelyn knows my penchant for saving the derelicts of the collectibles world, she decided to buy the lot for me if it brought under five dollars. The documents now are part of my collection.

Unknown to Jocelyn, I already owned several examples of old diplomas. I had been acquiring them over the years because I was fascinated with the engraving and the information that I found on them. I suppose the other reason that I have them is that I felt someone should be saving them, didn't know of anyone who was, and thought I had better stash a few until a dedicated collector for them arose.

Roland J. Wotring attended the North Whitehall Township School District in Lehigh Country, Pennsylvania. He completed his studies, with passing grades, in "Orthography, Reading, Writing, Written Arithmetic, Mental Arithmetic, English Grammar, Physiology, Geography, United States History, Physical Geography, Algebra, and Civil Government." I have seen some old diplomas with one or more of the subjects crossed out, obviously indicating a failure to pass. Roland received his diploma, a stock form issued by The Caxton Company of Chicago for various counties in the Commonwealth of Pennsylvania, at Schnecksville, on May 7, 1904.

Roland apparently had ambition. The second document is a certificate certifying him as a "Registered Qualified Assistant Pharmacist" issued in 1907. It was printed by Craig Finley & Co. of Philadelphia and lacks ornate calligraphy or nicely engraved vignettes.

The final document is a certificate noting Roland's admission to the Alumni Association of the Philadelphia College of Pharmacy as a member of the Class of 1909. The calligraphy on the top half of the certificate, done by John R. McFetridge & Sons Lithographers of Philadelphia, represents the epitome of the engraving art of that period.

Only recently have collectors begun to recognize the high level of skill exhibited by the engravers of the late nineteenth and early twentieth centuries. The broken banknote collectors, followed by the stock-and-bond certificate collectors, followed by the check collectors, have led the way to assembling information on the lithography and engraving firms of 1875 to 1915.

While information exists about some of the bigger firms, such as the American Banknote Company, not much is known about the secondary firms. But at least something is known. Rarely did an engraver sign a plate with other than the firm's name. Who actually did the work remains largely unknown.

As collectors discover the engraving art of 1875 to 1915, they will find an abundance of new examples in diplomas, membership certificates, confirmation and other religious materials, and business-related documents such as billheads and business cards. Initially the attraction is going to be the vignettes, as it is for the banknote, stock and bond, and check collectors. Eventually collectors will recognize the consummate skill required to do the lettering on the more elaborate certificates, making the most intricately done examples almost as valuable as the examples with the good vignettes.

Don't overlook diplomas and other engraved paper material from the point of view of the local collectible. Often these paper materials are one of the few survivals of a local institution that has vanished or changed its name. The North Whitehall Township School District that issued Wotring's diploma is now part of a much larger entity. The local collector is the traditionalist in our field, fighting to preserve the evidence that localism once had real meaning in American society.

Don't tell me this is not important. I attended Hellertown–Lower Saucon High School. I remember vividly the school assembly when we were told that the old name, Hellertown High School, was being dropped in the name of progress. The new name simply did not have the same sense of tradition as the old. Imagine my chagrin when the local school board built a new high school and called it Saucon Valley. I can feel no affinity with this school or its name. I didn't go there. I went to Hellertown–Lower Saucon. A great local tradition died, and no one seemed to care except for a few local collectors saving material with the old school names. I wonder if Roland Wotring felt the same way when his school district was merged and lost its identity?

The signatures on old diplomas and other certificates should not be overlooked. You are not likely to find an American president's signature unless you find a diploma from Princeton while Woodrow Wilson was president there. You will find plenty of local personalities, some of whom later gained fame outside their regions.

I look upon the signatures as a kind of challenge. Who were these people and what happened to them? Was serving on the local school board the high watermark of their career? With a little effort and a few old city or county directories, a good researcher can breathe some life back into these old names.

Well, where is all this leading? I am making a plea to auctioneers and estate executors to exhibit a little more concern for these paper products before they break up the accumulation of a lifetime. Try to find them a good home.

Why Not Football?

RECENTLY I attended an Antique Book, Paper, Advertising & Collectibles Show sponsored by Great Eastern Productions, Inc., in Allentown. As I was walking through the aisles, I spotted the board game "Ya-Lo: The Football Card Game," manufactured by the Ya-Lo Corporation, Columbus, Ohio, copyrighted in 1925, and dedicated to E. J. Graber, the originator. The price was only $15.

The game box measured 16 7/8" by 10". The multicolored lithograph cover shows a football game in progress as viewed from a grandstand containing a cheering crowd. The graphics are great.

The game consists of a game board in the shape of a playing field, a lead football to mark the location of play, a cardboard ten-yard marker, two packs of cards with one hundred cards in each pack (orange cards for the defense, blue cards for the offense), the original boxes for the cards, and an eight-page instruction booklet. Everything was there.

The edges of the box cover were frayed, and some well-intentioned soul applied tape to the tears on the edges to hold them together. But what started me thinking was a remark made by John Waldsmith, the dealer who sold me the game: "If this was a baseball game, I'd get $125 for it."

It is one of the realities in the collectibles field that football memorabilia simply does not sell as well as baseball memorabilia. In any given weekend, I can find a baseball card and memorabilia show to attend within a hundred-mile radius of my home. Baseball collectors have access to several independent price guides and newspapers. Football collectors have nothing.

Whenever I see football memorabilia at a modest price, especially if it dates before 1950, I acquire it for my collection. Personally, I think football memorabilia is very underpriced and not fully appreciated as a collectible. How do you explain the lack of a market?

I explored this question at length during a recent conversation with Don Raycraft, co-author along with Stew Salowitz of *Collector's Guide to Baseball Memorabilia* (Collector Books, 1986). Don and his sons are avid baseball collectors.

Don answered my question with a query of his own: "Did you ever have anyone try to sign a football? How many foul footballs are there?" Collectors love to have sports heroes sign an object associated with the sport. A professional football costs six to ten times that of a professional baseball. There are nets behind the goalposts for field goals and extra points because professional teams cannot afford to give away free footballs to the fans.

Don also suggested that baseball creates a greater number of heroes or individual superstars. Football still has not produced a superhero to rival the legend created by Babe Ruth. Football heroes are short-lived, baseball heroes are long-lived.

I think there is some truth to this. I am not an avid sports fan. But each year when the names of the inductees into the Baseball Hall of Fame are announced, I recognize them. When the inductees for the Football Hall of Fame are announced, I frequently ask myself: "Who? For whom did he play?" Yet, I watch far more football on television than I do baseball.

I also discussed the question of football versus baseball with Jerry Friedenheim, a friend and sometime sports enthusiast. Jerry feels that a typical baseball game contains far more action than a football game. Football is rather slow-paced. Only a few seconds of each play are devoted to actual action. The rest of the time is spent standing around or in huddles in a position in which most of us would not be caught dead in public.

Jerry also stressed the individuality of baseball. It's one man against another — the pitcher against the batter. The potential for a homerun exists each time the ball is thrown.

Football, especially in its modern form, is horribly complex. You hardly known who or what to watch. This is never a problem in baseball.

Finally, I think every American male has dreamed at one time or another of being a baseball hero and, whether on a sandlot or Little League diamond, probably fulfilled his fantasy. I never dreamed of being a football hero. I have this thing about self-inflicted physical abuse.

Football certainly has generated its share of collectibles. There are plenty of bubble-gum cards, team souvenirs, programs, and equipment. Collecting categories from match covers to games have football-related material dating back to the early 1900s.

A McDonald's promotion for the 1986–87 season includes pictures of some of the NFL superstars on cards. I already have added an example in my collection. If football memorabilia never catches on, I can have a shot with the card as a fast-food collectible.

What I think would be really neat is a collection of football memorabilia from all the professional and semiprofessional football teams and leagues that have folded. Have you ever heard of the Allentown Bulldogs? The apparent demise of the United States Football League offers a chance to get started now. I have letters on the way to USFL offices asking for some examples of their material for my collection.

Just one final thought. The fate suffered by football memorabilia is shared by memorabilia from other sports fields as well. Suppose you wanted a collection of autographed hockey pucks? How do you sign a little black hockey puck except in white, or maybe in red, like blood.

Anyone for tennis?

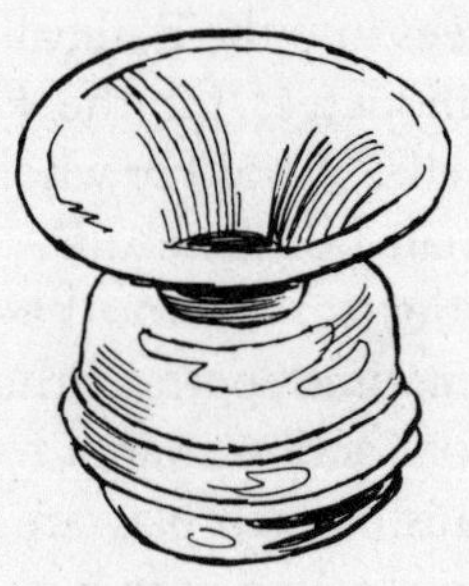

TV Games

ONE of the most heavily used reference books in my library is Tim Brooks and Earle Marsh's *The Complete Directory to Prime-Time Network TV Shows, 1946–Present* (Ballantine Books, 1981). The reason is simple. Many of the toys and games from the 1950s are television-related.

Material from the 1950s is now an established part of the collectibles market. It barely falls under Rinker's Thirty-Year Rule, but material from the 1950s is being actively traded. Prices are stable; in fact, they are showing steady signs of increase.

A major indication of the importance of the material from the 1950s is that the House of Collectibles has recently issued a price guide dealing specifically with that period. Charles J. Jordan's *The Official Price Guide to Collectibles of the '50s and '60s* offers an initial look at the broad spectrum of material that is attracting collector attention. The book's organization is a bit confusing. One chapter is entitled "What We Bought?" If you stop and think about it, we bought everything that appears in the book. I am not going to tell you what Jordan includes in this chapter. Maybe the suspense will tempt you to buy his book.

Nothing recaptures 1950s nostalgia for me more than the board games that were issued for the numerous television shows that aired then. But memories are only one of the reasons for my enthusiasm. The other is that the games are still modestly priced. Most games sell for under $40. Even the most expensive examples have not broken the $100 barrier.

TV games of the 1950s fall into several major categories—news-show games, children's show games, cowboy games, game-show games, and a miscellaneous assortment of games ranging from "Sherwood Forest" to the "Yukon." Each category evokes a different group of memories. "Return with us now to those thrilling days of yesteryear when . . ."

The news figures of the 1950s were larger than life. Two of the giants were John Cameron Swazye of NBC's Camel News Caravan and Dave Garroway of the Today Show. The "Swazye" game was issued by Milton Bradley in 1955, honoring the man who had pioneered the role of the television news anchor. Athletic Products Company produced the "Today with Dave Garroway" game in the mid-1950s. The game features metal television cameras as playing pieces.

The children of the 1950s were cowboy crazy. However, a few children's television shows defied this trend. Milton Bradley issued the "Howdy Doody T.V. Game" in 1950, Ewing "Davy Crockett" in 1955, Dexter Wayne "Ramar of the Jungle" in 1959, and Whiting "Pinky Lee Runaway Frankfurters" in 1954. If Howdy Doody, Clarabell, Phineas T. Bluster, and Princess Summerfallwinterspring marked the advent of the 1950s, the Mickey Mouse Club and Annette Funicello marked the end. Quite a contrast, isn't it?

Milton Bradley was the principal manufacturer of games that related to the television westerns of the 1950s. The company began with "Hopalong Cassidy" (1950) and followed with "Annie Oakley" (1955), "Cheyenne" (1958), "Rifleman" (1959), and "Tales of Wells Fargo" (1959). Lowell Toy Manufacturing Corporation kept pace with "Bat Masterson" (1958), "Gunsmoke" (1958), and "Laramie" (1959). Other television western games include "Boots and Saddles" (Gardner, 1958), "Life and Legend of Wyatt Earp" (Transogram, 1955), "Lone Ranger" (Whiting, 1956), "Rin-Tin-Tin" (Transogram, 1955), and "Wild Bill Hickock" (Bilt-Rite, 1956).

While children watched the western, the adults of the 1950s watched the game shows. The leading manufacturer was Lowell Toy Manufacturing Corporation, which issued "Beat the Clock" (1954), "Concentration" (1958), "I've Got a Secret" (1956), "The $64,000 Question Quiz Game" (1955), and "What's My Line?" (1955). A list of the emcees of these shows reads like a Who's Who of 1950s television: Bud Collyer from "Beat the Clock"; Jack Barry and Hugh Downs from "Concentration"; Gary Moore, Steve Allen, and Bill Cullen from "I've Got a Secret"; Hal March from "The $64,000 Question"; and, John Daly from "What's My Line?"

Yet these shows are only the tip of the iceberg. Other game shows resulting in board games include "Jan Murray's Treasure Hunt" (Gardner Games), "Tic-Tac Dough TV Game" (Transogram, 1957), "Name That Tune" (Milton Bradley, 1957), and the "Groucho TV Quiz Game" (Pressman, 1954). "Say the magic word and receive two hundred dollars."

Its hard to categorize the balance of the television show board games from the 1950s. The list is long. Comedy is represented by "Jackie Gleason, Away We Go" (Transogram, 1956) and "I'm George Goebel" (Highland Sales Company, 1955). "Dragnet" (Transogram, 1955) and "Perry Mason" (Transogram, 1959) cover the police and courtroom beat. The romantic adventure from Merry Olde England to outerspace encompasses "Bucanneers" (Transogram, 1957), "Robin Hood" (Betty-B, 1956), "Sgt. Preston" (Milton Bradley, 1956), and "Captain Video" (Milton Bradley, 1950).

In the 1950s the half-hour comedy series was still in its infancy. "You'll Never Get Rich" (Gardner, 1956) brought Sergeant Ernie Bilko from "The Phil Silvers Show" on to the family card or dining-room table. "This Is Your Life" (Lowell Toy Manufacturing Corporation) attempted to capture the emotionalism found in Ralph Edwards's show. However, nothing can beat "Lassie" (Whiting, 1955) for pure nostalgia. Who didn't love that show?

The dedicated television watchers of the 1950s should have tears in their eyes at this point. The names above represent a time lost in space, never to be recaptured again.

All that remains is to provide a few hints in case I have tempted you to begin collecting these games. First, make certain the box is in very good condition—all the sides intact, no scotch tape, and minimum surface dirt. No matter what is inside, it is generally the box lid that is displayed. Second, make certain the game is complete. The instructions usually include a list of game pieces. The instructions are especially important. What good is a game if you don't know how to play it?

Third, do not overpay. Remember, these games are not rare. They are not even scarce. There are plenty of examples both on the market and stored away in attics, closets, basements, and garages. If you buy an incomplete game merely to obtain spare playing pieces, never pay more than a few dollars.

Fourth, spread the word that you are looking for these games. They can still be found at garage, yard, and tag sales. Many individuals will gladly give them to you because you are willing to give them a good home. And make certain you do give them a good home. Don't stack more than three or four games on top of each other. A high stack will damage the games on the bottom. A friend cuts sheets of stiff, acid-free museum mat board and puts them between the games to distribute the weight load.

Finally, play with the games. Why not? The companies that manufactured them did not make them to be admired. Assuming you are adults and can play with your friends without seeking revenge from the winner by banging him or her over the head with a game board, you should be able to preserve the longevity and collectibility of the games.

Enough for now. I just received my first shipment of "Hopalong Cassidy" movies on VHS cassettes. In my life Hoppy movies come before everything else.

Old MacDonald had a Farm — Ee-igh, Ee-igh, Ohhhhh!

I am enamored with the agrarian myth. My ideal farm consists of a large farmhouse, a smaller grandparents' house, a huge bank barn with a silo, chicken coops, pigpens, corncribs, numerous outbuildings, and lots of equipment in sight. The scale of everything is large, oversized to tackle the tasks waiting to be done. Although well kept, the farm and all that it comprises has a well-worn look. The scene bespeaks generations — the family farm ennobled — a place loaded with potential collectibles.

Collectors have long identified the farm as one of the principal wellsprings for "original" antiques and collectibles. Traditionally, it has been the farmhouse that was raided. The contents of the barns, sheds, and outbuildings have been neglected, except by a few select collectors.

Farm collectibles simply have not developed as a separate and distinct collecting category. The collecting community accorded Lar Hothem's *Collecting Farm Antiques: Identification and Values* (Books Americana, 1982) a lukewarm response. The book deserved better.

The "country" look, more than anything else, has been responsible for the second-class status of farm collectibles. Country grew so inclusive that it absorbed the contents of the farmhouse, especially its parlor, kitchen, and bedroom. In many collectors' minds, the words "country" and "rural" are synonymous.

Examine the last several editions of Don and Carol Raycraft's *Wallace-Homestead Price Guide to American Country Antiques*. As you look at each object, ask one simple question: "Was this object predominately used on the farm or in the village?" Farm objects predominate. They may have been bought in the village store, but they were used on the farm.

Several "farm collectibles" categories have attracted attention, e.g., cast-iron implement seats, scales, tools, toy farm models, and windmill weights. Each has a collectors' club; several have specialized price guides.

The Cast Iron Seat Collectors Association (RFD 2, Box 40, Le Center MN 56057) was founded in 1973. Annual dues are $5.00. The membership rolls include individuals from the United States, Canada, Ireland, England, Australia, and New Zealand. The club has identified over 1,600 varieties of cast-iron seats. John Friedly Junior's *Cast Iron Seat Implement Seats IV* (available from the author at Box 14, Ionia, MN 65335) illustrates over 1,525 examples. Values range from $10 for a plain cast-iron seat to over $100 for an ornate seat with figural decoration.

The scale played an important part on any farm. My Uncle Kermit and Aunt Verna had an egg farm. Visits always included a session in the egg room using the egg scale to grade eggs. The Farm Master egg scale that I used has a current collectible value of over $30. The International Society of Antique Scale Collectors (20 N. Wacker Drive, Chicago, IL 60606) includes information about farm-related scales in its publication.

Collecting farm models (i.e., toys) has reached an advanced stage. Raymond E. Crilley and Charles E. Burkholder's *Collecting Model Farm Toys of the World* (Aztex Corporation, 1979) was the pioneering work. The book illustrates and describes farm toy models, past and present, from 24 countries. Crilley & Burkholder also authored *International Directory of Model Farm Tractors* for which a 1988-89 price guide is available. Dave Nolt's *Farm Toy Price Guide 1988 Edition* (P.O. Box 422, New Holland, PA 17557) is a computer generated listing of auction prices.

Three collector magazines fuel the market. *The Toy Farmer* (RR 2, Box 5, Lamoure, ND 58458) claims to be "the nation's most widely read farm toy magazine." A one-year subscription is $15. *The Toy Tractor Times* (P.O. Box 156, Osage, IA 50461-9635) has an annual subscription of $14. It reports auction results and activities at specialized collector shows. It also features a large classified advertising section and detailed listing of specialized shows. *Miniature Tractor & Implement* (1881 Eagley Road, East Springfield, PA 16411-9739), formerly *Toy Farm Equipment*, costs $15 annually. The magazines contain show advertisements, a calendar, and a small classified section.

Annual membership for the Ertl Replica Collector's Club (The ERTL Company, Highways 136 & 20, Dyersville, IA 52040) is $6 and includes *The Ertl Replica*, a newsletter giving information about The ERTL company's latest farm toys, cars, trucks, custom imprint banks, etc. The newsletter also has a calendar of shows, classified advertising, and information on collector's publications.

How big is the toy farm model collecting market? The National Farm Toy Show sponsored by *The Toy Farmer* and held annually in Dyersville, Iowa, normally draws between 18,000 and 20,000 collectors. No, I did not misplace the commas. The numbers are impressive.

A large variety of tools are an essential component of any farm. Ronald S. Barlow's *The Antique Tool Collector's Guide to Value* (Windmill Publishing Company, 1985) is the best source to identify and price tools. Tool Collectors unite in the Early American Industries Association (P.O. Box 2128, Empire Plaza Station, Albany, NY 12220). The Association's annual dues of $18 include *Shavings* (a bimonthly newsletter) and *The Chronicle* (a quarterly magazine).

The next time you see a windmill, check how it works. The blade is counterbalanced by a weight. Many of the old weights were figural or contained information about the maker. Donald E. Sites' *Windmills and Windmill Weights* (published by author, 1977) and Milt Simpson's *Windmill Weights* (Johnson & Simpson Graphic Designers in Association with the Museum of American Folk Art, 1985) are two books about windmill weight collecting. Unfortunately my information about Windmill Collectors (Box 7, W. T. Station, Canyon, TX 79016) is minimal, hence I do not know if the group deals with the history of windmills or windmill collectibles. I do know that the Windmill Study Unit (301 Thornbridge Drive, Midland, TX 79703) focuses on stamps dealing with windmills and related subjects.

Implement seats, scales, tools, toy farm models, and windmill weights only scratch the surface of farm collectibles. Unfortunately, collectors have relied on the state-operated farm museums, e.g., The Pennsylvania Farm Museum at Landis Valley, PA, to be the principal collectors and repositories for farm material. While the efforts of these museums are commendable, they are not enough. We need more collectors interested in farm-related categories.

Earlier I mentioned the problem of size. A farm collector needs storage space—*lots* of storage space. You cannot put ten wooden fanning mills or manure spreaders in your living room. This problem does not stop antique and classic car collectors. It should not deter the collector of farm memorabilia.

Farm collectors unite. Let's give farm collectibles a proper roost in the collecting community.

Limited-Edition Anything

THE letter sounds wonderful, almost too good to be true. "In recent years, Reco International has made consistent headlines with the success of its first-issue, child-subject collector plates. . . . First-issue, child-subject plates from Reco and from many other makers—especially those with nostalgic themes like 'School Days'—have dominated the plate market over the past decade . . . [a list of five plates all increasing more than five times in value follows]. . . . Based on the success of Reco's child-subject plates, their unprecedented range of awards, and more specifically the recent success of the nostalgic 'Sunday Best' plate, it is likely that the new 'School Days' plate will become a big market success, as well."

The name on the envelope might be the Bradford Exchange, the Franklin Mint, the Hamilton Collection, or one of more than a hundred companies specializing in the sale of limited-edition collectibles. The real question is: Is the object likely to appreciate in value? The basic answer is no.

If you buy a limited-edition collectible because you like its aesthetic appeal and want to enjoy it for years to come, you are a realist. If you are buying a limited-edition collectible because you want to make money, your odds are better at the racetrack or in the casinos in Atlantic City or Las Vegas.

Limited-edition collectible promoters have tempered the language of their pitch letters in recent years. However, one has to take a "what does it really mean?" attitude when evaluating the claims. A typical letter from the Bradford Exchange provides several examples:

1. "True collector plates . . . are produced in strictly limited editions. Once that limit is reached, the edition is closed and no more plates can ever be made." How do you define limited: 1,000, 5,000, 10,000, or more? A production run of 5,000 is not limited. This is mass-production. In many cases, limited editions are limited to exactly how many people are willing to buy them.

2. "Are there any collector's plates that qualify not just as decorative objects, but as true works of art? . . . Yes." This is certainly an optimistic answer. No artist is going to sit around and hand-paint the same design on 5,000 or more items. The design is placed on the object either by a transfer process or by someone interpreting the prototype. Have you ever seen a limited-edition collectible hanging on the wall of an art museum? You might see the original work of art from which the design was copied, but you will never see the product itself.

This is not to suggest that some of the designs on limited-edition collectibles are not aesthetically pleasing. Some are rather attractive. In making an evaluation, however, do not confuse nostalgia for aesthetics. Even Norman Rockwell had a bad day.

3. "And you stand to gain monetarily as well as to meet exhilarating challenges as you learn to play the ups and downs of the marketplace." It is an honest statement on two counts.

First, if you are going to invest in limited-edition material, you have to play a game. Its name is market manipulation. You can count on the manufacturer to promote the product only during its initial stage of production. Long-term promotion is left to the collector.

Second, the Bradford Exchange letter admits the market goes down as well as up. You had better believe it does. In fact, the value of most limited-edition items goes down and stays down. It is an exception, not the rule, when something increases above its initial purchase value and retains that value.

If you stop to think about it, the prevailing decreasing trend makes sense. The final selling price of any limited-edition collectible has profit in it for somebody, in many cases several individuals. Assume that over half the price you pay is profit.

When you buy a car, you accept the fact that when you drive it out of the showroom, you can only recover about fifty percent of the price you paid if you were forced to sell it a month later. The same holds true for furniture and a wealth of other products. Collectors must view limited-edition collectibles in the same light.

Remember Rinker's Thirty-Year Rule. When you buy a limited-edition collectible, you are speculating. No ifs, ands, or buts. You are speculating, pure and simple.

The true value of any limited-edition collectible is what you can get for it if you have to sell it, not what a replacement costs at market value. The big problem with the limited-edition market is that there is no firmly established resale market. Collectors are on their own.

If you do not believe me, try selling a limited-edition collectible. Call the Bradford Exchange or the manufacturer and see if they would like to buy it back. Chances are the answer is an emphatic no. Their role is making and selling the product, not maintaining a secondary market.

Try advertising your limited-edition collectible in your local paper or one of the trade papers merely for the price you paid for it. You are likely to die of old age waiting for the first phone call unless, of course, you were lucky and bought one of those rare limited-edition collectibles that did go up in value. Is the gamble worth it?

I recommend that manufacturers issue a crying towel with each limited-edition collectible so collectors have something with which to dry their eyes just in case their object fails to yield a return and they are faced squarely with a loss. If anyone is likely to make a long-term profit on limited-edition collectibles, it will be the grandchildren or great-grandchildren of the original purchaser.

I am not advocating that you refrain from buying limited-edition collectibles. If you do buy them, do so with your eyes and mind wide open. Buy them for decorative purposes or as family keepsakes that you will pass down from generation to generation. Do not buy them as investments.

The fifth edition of Gene Ehlert's *The Official Price Guide to Collector Plates* (House of Collectibles, 1988), presents a "positive" pitch for limited-edition collectibles in a lengthy introduction to his pricing guide. Paul Stark's *Limited Edition Collectibles: Everything You Really Should Know* (New Gallery Press: 1988) falls in the same vein. Both are well worth reading. After thinking about both sides, make up your own mind. That is what life is all about.

Let's Collect the Losers

ONE of my employees was sorting through a collection of political buttons relating to the 1972 presidential campaign when she spotted a pinback jugate for McGovern and Eagleton. The button was not issued when Senator Thomas F. Eagleton of Missouri was officially on the Democratic ticket, but as a collector's item at a later date.

"What's this?" she asked, "I thought McGovern's running mate was Shriver." She was a young teenager at the time of the election, and this footnote in history simply had not become part of her permanent memory.

Then it occurred to me. Collectibles collectors are not interested in the losers. They want to collect the winners. Is it possible they are overlooking something important?

There is no bigger area of losers than in the political arena. You can interpret this remark anyway you like. Have you ever heard of William Jennings Bryan, Alton B. Parker, Charles Evans Hughes, James M. Cox, or Alfred E. Smith? They were all major-party candidates for president of the United States. What about Eugene Victor Debs, Robert M. LaFollette, Norman Thomas, J. Strom Thurmond, Henry A. Wallace, or Harry F. Byrd? They all ran for the presidency between 1920 and 1956 and garnered more than 200,000 votes in an election.

It doesn't take much imagination to realize that campaign items and other materials associated with the losers are much scarcer than that associated with the winners. People save things associated with winners; they throw out things associated with losers. Since the material is scarcer and much harder to find, it seems logical to conclude that it is more valuable. Wrong, wrong, wrong!

People save what they remember, and they remember winners. Collecting things associated with winners makes the collector feel good. It is a positive approach. Collecting things relating to losers has a negative connotation.

Being branded common is almost as bad as being branded a loser. The baseball card collectors provide an excellent example of this phenomenon. The baseball collector tends to concentrate on the star players, those individuals who are potential Hall of Fame candidates. The ordinary players that had so-so statistics and lasted only a few months or years are forgotten and lumped together in the general classification of common players.

In the 1960 set of Topps baseball cards, common players on cards numbered 1 through 506 sell for 25¢ each. Common players on cards numbered 507 to 572 sell for 90¢ each. Although common, there must be something a bit uncommon about this latter group to make them sell for an additional 65¢ each. In the same series, Carl Yastrzemski's rookie card (No. 148) lists at $45, Hank Aaron's (No. 300) at $11, and Mickey Mantle's (No. 350) at $20.

In August 1986 I attended the national convention of the Rathkamp Matchcover Society. A match-cover album filled with covers of baseball and hockey stars from the 1930s was offered at auction. When the bidding was done, a collector had purchased the album at an average price of slightly over $1 per cover. What a bargain, I thought. It was a shame that some baseball collectors were not there. They would have blown that match-cover collector right out of the water.

Well, as you know by now, I am never content to let an idea go until I have followed it through. Within the week, I was talking to my friends who are baseball collectors to find out if these sports match covers had interest to them. The answer startled me.

Time and again I heard the same response. "No, I don't collect them. They have too many common players and not enough stars in the series." The match company could not afford to pay a big royalty, and many of the star players of the time would not agree to allow their pictures to be used. One collector said he had more than 2,000 of the match covers in his basement. He would supply me with as many as I wanted at a $1 a cover.

How often have you heard the phrase, "it's so rare, I've never seen one before?" Usually, it's said by sellers who are trying to justify a high price for something. But in reality are they simply trying to prop up a loser?

Maybe the reason a piece is so rare is that few people wanted it when it was made, and nobody with any collecting sense wants it now. If collectors would consider this second alternative each time they look at a "rare" object, they might save themselves a considerable amount of money.

Have you ever tried to look up something associated with a loser? As I write, I'm trying to check the correct spelling of Senator Eagleton's name. The political button books don't have the jugate pictured because it was a collectors' item and not an actual campaign item. Reference books listing presidential candidates and the results of their elections record the candidates as they stood on election night. I know my local library has a biographical compendium of all the individuals who served in the U.S. House of Representatives and Senate. But this does you little good at nine o'clock on a Sunday night.

Thus far, I have confined my discussion of losers to real people and political parties. But this is only the tip of the iceberg. If you had a team from the United States Football League in your area, I hope you had stashed a few promotional relics away for the future. What about all those dolls that were issued in 1984 when the Cabbage Patch craze hit that no one bought? Better save a few.

Of course, I realize that this can get carried to extremes. I am not advocating saving paintings on velvet of JFK, Elvis, or Martin Luther King, crocheted toilet-paper covers in the shape of hats that are found in bathrooms across the nation, or paintings by unknown local artists that are sold in galleries located in bank lobbies or restaurants. No, I'm not advocating you should save these things. I don't want to undercut the value of my own collection.

Lunch Boxes

INSTEAD of bronzing a child's first pair of shoes, parents who want to preserve a major milestone in their child's development should bronze their first lunch box. The lunch box represents one of the earliest attempts by a child to express his or her own creativity. The child influences the purchase. Until a lunch box is bought, the child has been the pawn of parental selection and television advertising. The child's clothes, toys, and cereal have all been manipulated by the aspiration of parents, along with food and toy manufacturers.

But there are few advertisements for lunch boxes. The child usually makes the selection independent of outside forces. It is the wise parent who lets a child do this. Few children are willing to carry their lunch to school, picnics, or other events in a lunch box that does meet with their approval. The lunch box makes a statement.

The selection of a lunch box is serious business. Most children carry lunch boxes featuring a popular movie or television cartoon character or personality. At first glance, it appears to be hero worship. But look closely. The character or personality selected may also express how the child perceives his future self. It does not take a genius to figure out there is a big difference between a "Mr. T" lunch box and a Smurf lunch box.

Once a child selects a lunch box, he or she is likely to continue using it for years. Lunch boxes are surprisingly durable. It is not a common practice to buy a new one for a child at the beginning of each school year. Except for a few select toys, the lunch box is one of the permanent aspects of childhood.

Lunch boxes are sexist. If you don't believe me, shop around and look at the selection. Visit your local elementary school and see the type of lunch boxes carried by boys and girls. It is an unusual male that will carry his lunch to school in a Miss Piggy lunch box.

By the time a child becomes a teenager, the lunch box becomes passé. It is relegated to the basement, closet, garage, or trash can. When the child reaches his thirties and finds an example of his old lunch box at a flea market or antiques show, it evokes nostalgic memories of childhood heroes and peanut butter and jelly sandwiches. In almost every instance, the temptation to repurchase this memento is irresistible.

Lunch box collecting on a serious scale began in the early 1980s. In 1982 *The Paileontologist's Retort*, a newsletter for lunch box collectors was launched. It has been replaced today by *Hot Boxing*, a quarterly newsletter available from editor Scott Bruce, P.O. Box 87, Somerville, MA 02143. *Hot Boxing* contains information about the design history of lunch boxes, historical data, classified ads, and trivia.

You probably were unaware that while there was no "Leave It to Beaver" lunch box, one episode did show the Beaver leaving his home with a 1957 Tweed Luggage lunch box made by American Thermos. But mystery prevails. Since the model was made in three color combinations and the show was in black and white, collectors are unable to determine the exact lunch box the Beaver carried.

Today's lunch box collectors have little interest in the nineteenth-century tin lunch boxes used by factory workers and fieldhands. They prefer the decorated and illustrated child's lunch boxes that date from the late 1930s to the present. Among the earliest boxes is a No. 9100 Mickey Mouse lunch kit issued by Gender, Paeschke & Frey Company of Milwaukee, Wisconsin, for the 1935 Christmas trade. An oval lunch box of a streamlined train, marked "Decoware," dates from the same period.

The two leading manufacturers of lunch boxes are Aladdin and King Seeley, formerly the American Thermos Company. Other manufacturers include Adco Liberty; Landers, Frary and Clark; Ohio Art (successor to Hibbard, Spencer, Bartlett & Company), and Universal. Actually, the collector cares little about the manufacturer.

The keys to lunch box collecting are the design motif, condition, and completeness. The design is everything. Unfortunately, every design attracts a collector from another category, thus creating direct competition with the lunch box collector. For examples, an Aladdin Jetson lunch box will attract the cartoon-character collector, outer-space collector, 1950s collector, and Jetson collector in addition to the lunch box collector. In most cases, these specialized collectors will pay more for the box than the lunch box collector.

It is for this reason that the lunch box collector haunts the garage sales, church rummage sales, and flea markets. If the collector hopes to build a significant collection at a modest price, he must find the boxes when they first appear on the market. In many cases, the collector will buy duplicates. Swapping is a common practice among serious collectors.

A survey of *Hot Boxing's* members showed that approximately 40 collectors owned close to 10,000 lunch boxes. The average collection size was 250 boxes. It was estimated that the total membership has more than 30,000 lunch boxes in their possession. Sounds like a lot, doesn't it? Not really. Many of the early lunch boxes were manufactured in the tens of thousands. There are a lot of old lunch boxes yet to be uncovered.

Once a lunch box has begun to rust, or the surface design has been badly scratched, contains dents, or is covered with stickers, it is a lost cause. One might as well scrap the box. Since lunch boxes are purchased primarily for display purposes and their market value remains modest, collectors will continue to search until they find a box in near-perfect condition rather than settle for a badly damaged one.

A dangerous collecting trend, fostered to some extent by greedy dealers, is to separate the thermos from a child's lunch box and sell it as a separate item. Many vacuum bottles also contain a decorative motif related to the lunch box theme. Some dealers have been asking as much for the vacuum bottle as they do for the box. A lunch box without its appropriate vacuum bottle is incomplete. The trend can be stopped if collectors simply refuse to buy a lunch box without its vacuum bottle.

A sampling of lunch box prices from the third edition of *Warman's Americana & Collectibles* includes Gene Autry (Adco Liberty, 1950s) at $50; Adam 12 (Aladdin, 1972) at $10; Beatles' Yellow Submarine (King Seeley, 1969) at $100; James Bond (Aladdin, 1966) at $40; Get Smart (King Seeley) at $25; Flying Nun (Aladdin, 1968) at $15; Kung Fu (King Seeley, 1974) at $5; Osmonds (Aladdin, 1973) at $10; Partridge Family (King Seeley, 1971) at $5; and, Wild, Wild West (Aladdin, 1969) at $30.

Since lunch box collecting is still a relatively new collecting category, prices do fluctuate, especially for lunch boxes dating after the mid-1960s. Although collectors continue to concentrate on the lithographed tin boxes, a growing interest is being shown in the vinyl boxes.

A new collector is well advised to develop a specialized theme, such as television cowboy shows, movies, or Disneyana. It pays to keep a "handle" on the size of your collection. Fifty-plus lunch boxes take up a lot of room.

Giving a Toot!

I played the trumpet. Note the use of the past tense. I stopped playing the trumpet during my junior year in college when I found that I was a good second-rate trumpet player and that good second-rate trumpet players were a dime a dozen. I think they still are.

The key point is that while I quit playing the trumpet, I did not give up my trumpet. My trumpet, its accessories, and music moved from Hellertown to Allentown, St. Louis, Bethlehem, York, Hellertown, Bethlehem, and finally Zionsville. It was a well-traveled instrument. My trumpet was a personal appendage. Getting rid of it was equivalent to cutting off an arm or a leg. Life seemed incomplete without it.

Since I began my music lessons in sixth grade at the age of eleven and I am now forty-six, my trumpet falls under Rinker's Thirty-Year Rule. At this point, my trumpet should be a collectible. Right? Wrong!

In the collectibles field, there are a few categories—musical instruments is one of them—where the value of the object rests more with its usability than with its collectibility. There is an active market in secondhand musical instruments. Music stores often buy them for use as rental instruments. Parents of budding musicians buy them to postpone the purchase of a new instrument until they determine the seriousness of their children's interest.

Think about it. What would you do with twenty Sousaphones or saxophones? The problem with musical instruments is that you can only play one at a time. From an aesthetic point of view, most musical instruments leave much to be desired. I've never met a piano case I wanted to caress. It is the *sound* the instrument makes that fascinates the musician.

In the past, musicians, museums, and music school archives have been the principal players in the antique and collectible musical-instrument field. A long-standing tradition among violinists asserts that antique instruments by makers such as Stradivarius produce the quality tones. A number of antique violins have broken the $100,000 barrier.

Within the past several years, a number of nonmusician collectors have been attracted to musical instruments. These new collectors are fascinated by the evolution in design of musical instruments. As new material and new technology arise, musical instruments change. Sometimes the changes are subtle. In other cases, the changes are dramatic. The use of metal in place of wood for flutes is one example.

Leading the effort to attract attention to the collectibility of all types and periods of musical instruments is Glenn M. Kramer, a consultant to Doyle Auctioneers and Appraisers (R.D. 3, Box 137, Fishkill, NY 12524). Glenn organizes a minimum of two musical-instrument auctions a year for Dolye's. For the first time there is an auction house, outside the rarified atmosphere of the major New York auction houses, that is willing to offer instruments in the middle and low end of the market. The importance is that these instruments are no longer viewed as "secondhand" but as potential collectibles.

A recent sale featured the following: a King tenor saxophone, serial number 271360, at $195; a Selmer "Signet" flute, serial number 346679, at $170; a German flugel horn at $100; a tenor "Gretsch Broadcaster" banjo, serial number 1480, at $65; a Brandt bowl mandolin, style "O", serial number 8348, c. 1915, at $85; and, a "Tivoli" button accordion at $75. Now these are hardly huge sums, but they represent a significant improvement over the $10 to $25 that you can obtain for the same instruments at a garage sale or flea market.

The Doyle sale featured a wide variety of musical instruments, instrument parts and accessories, and memorabilia. Instruments included clarinets, French horns, flutes, guitars, sousaphones, trombones, trumpets, ukeleles, violins, zithers, and many more. Memorabilia covered advertising items, music books, phonographs, posters, and even a statue of Nipper.

Good information about a collectible is always a key to attracting interest to that category. For the past six years, the House of Collectibles' *Official Price Guide to Music Collectibles* has served as an important source of information for musical instruments at all price levels. The strength of the book rests with its introduction and the introductory notes appearing with each collecting category. The book is one of the few places that you can find price information for accordions, drums, harmonicas, mandolins, pianos, and ukeleles, as well as the more conventional instruments.

Before you head for the closet and dig out that vestige of your musical past, remember two things. First, be honest when you appraise its condition. A musical instrument that is no longer playable has very little value. Second, no collectible has value until you find a buyer. The collectible market for musical instruments is still in its infancy. It currently is a buyer's, not a seller's, market. Do not expect to make a killing on a sale. On the other hand, some money is better than no money.

I return to my trumpet for one last time, if nothing more than to evoke the nostalgic memories it holds for me. You see, I no longer own it. No, I didn't sell it. I was too dumb. Instead, I gave it to my cousin's son. I guess I finally just didn't give a toot!

All the News That's Fit to Collect

YOUNG collectors are always looking for something to collect that is affordable, easy to store, has good historical content, and displays pizzazz. One obvious answer is newspapers.

The newspaper market, especially for twentieth-century material, is still in its infancy. Phil Barber (Box 8694, Boston, MA 02114), has put together a wonderful twelve-page booklet entitled "Collecting Historic Newspapers: An Introduction." It is a must for the beginning collector.

Phil issues a regular catalog that concentrates on eighteenth- and nineteenth-century newspapers. The news it contains is terrific. First, there is a wide variety of material available to the collector. Second, the material is affordable. There are bargains galore below $50, with many papers priced in the $5 to $15 range.

A good basic, starting collection can be assembled for a few hundred dollars, especially if the collector narrows his concentration when beginning. In his booklet, Phil notes that possible collecting themes are advertisements, correspondents (Mark Twain, Karl Marx, Winston Churchill, and Winslow Homer all wrote for newspapers), editors, eras (Civil War, Prohibition), famous events and headlines, first editions, mastheads, and the first appearance of famous literary works. This list only scratches the surface.

I collect material relating to the American canal system. Newspapers that chronicle the annual rates of tolls on the canals, advertisements for shippers and the arrival of canalboats, records of breaks and accidents, and the closing of canals are part of my collection. In fact, Dorothy Sanderson compiled a book on the Delaware and Hudson Canal that consisted primarily of newspaper extracts about events along the canal during its period of operation.

But enough of this nineteenth-century emphasis. *Rinker on Collectibles* is about twentieth-century material. What are the secrets for collecting modern newspapers?

My good friend Tim Hughes (2410 North Hills Drive, Williamsport, PA 17701) is most responsible for turning me on to twentieth-century newspapers. I came into contact with Tim because I found a variety of headline newspapers when I was going through my mother's estate. Either my dad or mom saved the papers when World War II ended, when Eisenhower was elected president, when John F. Kennedy was shot, and many more. I asked Tim if they had any value and what I should do with them.

First, Tim pointed out to me that most twentieth-century newspapers were printed on newsprint made from a combination of chemicals and woodpulp that self-destructs and eventually turns to yellow and brown unless you take care to preserve them.

The natural enemies of newspapers are excessive heat, humidity, and sunlight. Most collectors store their newspapers flat and encase them in an airtight wrapper such as Mylar. They select a relatively cool, dry place that is away from sunlight, heat sources, and leaky water pipes. A number of collectors deacidify their papers to increase their life.

Again turn to Phil Barber's excellent introductory pamphlet for a list of sources for the supplies a collector needs to do it right. Mylar sleeves are available from Cohasco, Inc., P.O. Box 821, Yonkers, NY 10702; deacidifiers and other supplies from American Library Service Corp., 2360 West Granville Road, Worthington, OH 43085; and a general line of archival supplies from University Products, Inc., P.O. Box 101, Holyoke, MA 01041.

If you are going to frame your newspapers, make certain to use acid-free mats and UF–3 or equivalent Plexiglas, one that filters out harmful light rays. Make certain you do not hang the framed paper on a wall that is exposed to sunlight.

Second, Tim notes that the rules for collecting are relatively simple and based on common sense. All newspapers must be in one piece with a minimum amount of chipping and cracking. The front page commands sixty percent of the value of the newspaper since the headline is the drawing point in most twentieth-century collections.

A newspaper headline has more value when it appears on the masthead of a newspaper published in the city where the event happened. The November 23, 1963, issue of the *New York Times* with the headline of the Kennedy assassination is worth $18, but the copy of the *Dallas Herald* of the same date is worth $36.

Twentieth-century headline newspapers are surprisingly reasonable. The stock market crash edition of October 28, 1929, sells for $30; the Alaskan statehood edition of June 30, 1958, for $15, and the death of Elvis edition of August 16, 1977, for $10. But don't be fooled. There are a few expensive papers in the pile. A December 17, 1903, paper recording the Wright Brothers first flight is in the $175 to $200 range. The November 3, 1948, "Dewey Defeats Truman" paper sells for $600 plus.

How about your birthdate? When I go to fairs, the shore, or trade shows, I almost always run across a booth wishing to supply you with a replica paper with the headline from the day of your birth. Why settle for second best? A good dealer such as Phil or Tim can supply you with the real thing at far less money, unless you have the misfortune of being born on the day the *Titanic* sank.

Collecting newspapers will turn you into a historian. You have a piece of living history. Tim Hughes loves to tell the story of his conversion from a coin collector to newspaper collector and dealer. "One day I was at a flea market and saw a newspaper from the early 1800s for $3.00. I brought it home and started to read it. I was so excited. I was reading an eyewitness account of history. I realized that here was a hobby that was affordable and as historically impressive as coins."

Newspaper collectors love to share this enthusiasm and what they have with each other. The National Association of Newspaper Collectors (P.O. Box 19134, Lansing, MI 48901) publishes "Collectible Newspapers" six times a year. The annual subscription is $15.

Collecting old newspapers is like horse racing. Everyone has his or her own favorite. All the news that's fit to collect can range from the historic to the tragic, from the exotic to the erotic. Whatever turns you on!

"I've Got a Collection of 78 rpm Records and . . ."

I just missed the era of the 78 rpm record. I was a teenager in the 1950s, and by that time the 45 rpm record was king. This is not to say that the 78 rpms did not play a vital role in my life. I broke my share of 78s by tossing a baseball at them attempting to win prizes at the local fireman's carnival.

However, for the generations growing up from 1915 until 1950, the 78 rpm record was a vital source of musical enjoyment, from jazz to the classics. People who grew up with the music of the 78s loved the songs and the sounds. Collections were retained long after technology made them obsolete. Most of today's record players do not even contain the means for playing 78 rpm records.

About once a week, I receive a letter from someone who has a collection of old 78 rpm records and wonders what to do with them. Do they have any value? How can I sell them? Surprisingly enough, there is a wealth of collectors seeking old 78 rpm records. There are papers and other means through which they can be bought and sold easily.

First, a few pieces of advice about the records themselves. Condition is everything. Collectors want records in very good or better condition. A very good record has some wear, slight grayness in the grooves, and, while surface and extraneous noise is noticeable, it does not overwhelm the music. An excellent record retains much of its original shine on the playing surface and surface noise is minimal. Records in good condition (with random mars and light abrasions) and below are difficult to sell and often are simply junked. Only the rarest records sell in these grade levels.

Second, records generally were pressed in the tens of thousands or more. The chances of you having a rare recording are slim. It pays to check, but learn to be honest with yourself when evaluating a 78 rpm record collection.

Third, most 78 rpm records still fall in a price range below $5. Extremely common records, such as Bing Crosby's recording of "White Christmas," are worthless. Dealers and collectors buying large collections still pay 25¢ to $1 per record.

Fourth, there is a pecking order. Classical records may indicate a high-brow refinement, but they do not reflect a high-brow price. The collecting categories that produce the best prices are jazz, big bands, blues, and some Country & Western material.

Getting some idea of price is simple. There are three basic books: L. R. Docks's *American Premium Record Guide: Identification and Value Guide to 1915–1965 78s, 45s, and LPs*, third edition (Books Americana, 1986), Peter A. Soderbergh's *Dr. Records' Original 78 RPM Price Guide* (Wallace-Homestead, 1983); and Peter A. Soderbergh's *Olde Records Price Guide, 1900–1947: Popular and Classical 78 RPM'S* (Wallace-Homestead, 1983). Two books by Jerry Osborne and Bruce Hamilton, *Record Album Price Guide*, fourth edition, and *Movie/TV Soundtracks & Original Cast Albums Price Guide*, do contain a few 78 rpm references, but they concentrate more on 45 rpm and long-play records.

The best news of all is that record collectors now have their own twice-monthly newspaper devoted to the buying and selling of records, with 78 rpms playing a major role. *Goldmine* is published by Krause Publications (700 East State Street, Iola, WI 54990). A one-year subscription of twenty-six issues costs $35.

Goldmine provides the addresses of the major record dealers in the United States, informative articles and columns on record history, lists of regional conventions of record collectors (a sample issue for June 1984 contained more than fifty such meetings spanning a two-month period), several mail auctions, and a large classified advertising section.

Each issue, done on newsprint, now averages well over one hundred pages. If you have records you want to buy or sell, you can do it through this source. *Goldmine* focuses primarily on records from the 1920s and 1930s to the present, increasing its emphasis over the past years in the 45 rpm and long-play categories. It is not a good source for the early material, such as Edison disks.

Goldmine now has a rival, *Discoveries* (P.O. Box 255, Port Townsend, WA 98368). The annual subscription to *Discoveries* is $12.

Stores specializing in the sale of old 78 rpm records do exist in towns such as Chicago, Detroit, Fort Worth, Glendale (California), San Diego, and elsewhere. A few specialized record flea markets are held, especially in California. The only thing the potential buyer or seller needs to know about these flea markets is that trading begins about midnight and frequently is over by the early morning hours. Don't plan to arrive late.

Dr. H. A. Hyman's *Cash for Your Undiscovered Treasures!*, third edition (Treasure Hunt Publications, 1986), contains three pages of individuals who are willing to purchase various types of 78 rpm records. Several things can be noted from the listing. First, most buyers on Hyman's list want to buy large collections, 1,000 record minimum and collections over 5,000 records preferred. Some will respond to a list of single offerings if you enclose a stamped, self-addressed return envelope. Second, the average purchase price ranges from 10¢ to $1 maximum per record. *Shellac Shack's Wants List*, a seventy-two-page booklet listing 78 rpm records that the firm will buy, can be obtained by sending $2 to Shellac Shack, Box 32924, San Antonio, TX 78216.

I think it's fair to state that 78 rpm collectors are no longer in the majority among the record collectors. Today the collectors of 45 rpm and LP records constitute the major portion of the market. However, those old 78s still have value. Before you decide to go into the carnival concession business with your collection, check into some of the sources that I have listed.

If all else fails, buy an old 78 rpm record player, prop up your feet, and listen to the music. The memories it will invoke will be well worth the expenditure for the player.

Oh, Sheet . . .

AMONG the happiest of my childhood memories is the absence of piano lessons. This is not to suggest that my musical education was neglected. I became a fairly competent trumpet player through repeated practice and a willingness to march in my winter band uniform, the only one that was provided, in summer parades and up and down muddy football fields in all types of inclement fall weather.

In the intervening years, I developed a love and appreciation for great music, skillfully performed. I am horrified every time I think of the quality of the music my parents endured as they listened to their son and his contemporaries blow and toot their brains out. I understood so well that I encouraged my children *not* to take up a musical instrument. Relying on the high-volume screech of radio, MTV, and "Friday Night Videos," my children achieved an even greater level of parental abuse without the endless hours of practice. Is there no justice in this world?

My trumpet, along with its mutes, music stand, and other accessories, is long gone. However, I recently rediscovered the box containing my trumpet sheet music. It was then that I wished I had played the piano. The covers of my trumpet sheet music were plain and lifeless. They had none of the pizzazz of piano sheet music, and none of its potential value.

Sheet music has been an established collectible for several decades. Collectors actually fall into two groups—those who collect the sheets because of the cover design, and those who collect the sheets because of the music title. Both groups compete with specialized collectors from other collecting categories who are seeking a specific song or cover design to enhance their collection. In most cases, the specialized collector is prepared to outbid the sheet music collector.

Reality dictates that every sheet music collector become a specialist in their own right. More than three million songs have been written and published. No collector can hope to assemble a copy of every one. In some cases, hundreds of cover variations may exist for a single title. The collecting possibilities are almost limitless.

It also must be understood that the normal press run for a song's sheet music often numbers in the tens of thousands of copies. The large printings of World War I and World War II sheet music continue to keep its price in the modest range. When a song became popular, more and more sheets were printed. Sheet music for the songs that everybody sang and played exists in such large quantity that they have little or no value. An excellent example is "White Christmas."

This is not to say that all sheet music has limited value. If you find a copy of the first printing of Irving Berlin's "Marie from Sunny Italy," his first song, in very good condition, you have a treasure worth in excess of $5,000. The sheet music cover for H. R. Hempel's "Cubs on Parade," dedicated to Franch Chance, sold for $360 at the October 15, 1988, Phillips' Lead Soldiers, Toys, and Sports Memorabilia auction. The cover featured a line of dancing teddy bears. Covers issued by E. T. Paull with vivid designs are worth hundreds of dollars.

However, the vast majority of sheet music is worth very little. Values range from 10¢ to $3 to $5 per sheet. Buying and selling sheet music is labor-intensive. Someone has to sort the stuff. A dealer who offers an individual twenty-five to fifty cents per sheet for a large collection coming out of a basement or attic is probably making a fair offer. In some cases, the person may increase the offer to $1 per sheet, provided he can pick and choose.

When a dealer buys an entire collection, a high percentage is usually discarded, such as sheet music of popular songs that is torn, repaired with tape, has pages missing, or features plain covers. Collectors want examples in very good or better condition. Most individuals who discover a collection greatly overestimate the condition of the individual sheets. A tear, creased and crinkled paper, damaged edges and sides, or handwritten notes (especially on the cover) quickly downgrade the condition.

Dealers have difficulty selling the sheet music of popular songs for much more than a few dollars. Think for a minute. What prompted the person to buy the sheet music in the first place? In most cases, it was the popularity of the song. Therefore, it is safe to assume that the songs found in most household collections are the most common ones.

Identifying the scarcity of a piece of sheet music is difficult unless you are totally familiar with the market. What may appear rare may in fact be quite common. Collectors are frustrated by the large number of common sheets that are marked with high values. Do not pay a high price for any sheet music until you understand the rarity issue.

Sheet music with a Black theme, whether in text or cover design, is a case in point. It has been rising in value over the past decade. Serious sheet music collectors know that there are more than a hundred very common Black songs and covers. Their value is minimal. Yet many dealers who handle sheet music as a sideline place a premium value on any Black song or cover regardless of whether it is common or rare. Novice and less knowledgeable collectors who pay the price discover later the error of their ways.

Anyone who purchases a large sheet music collection must invest considerable time and money in finding the right buyers for specific pieces. This means incurring the overhead to attend and sell at mall and specialized shows, advertising in trade papers, and writing to a variety of collectors whose specialized needs are on file.

Sheet music does offer the potential to build a large, exciting, and focused collection for a minimal investment. The more expensive categories currently include sheet music with ragtime, baseball, political, Black, and scarcer Walt Disney (not "Someday My Prince Will Come") themes. Categories rising in value are covers featuring silent movie songs and stars, Art Deco and 1940s motifs, and 1950s Rock'n'Roll featuring artists such as Little Richard, Chuck Berry, and Bill Haley.

There are several sheet music collectors' clubs. Before you begin collecting or dealing in sheet music, you are well advised to join several of them. The clubs include National Sheet Music Society (1597 Fair Park Avenue, Los Angeles, CA 90041), New York Sheet Music Society (c/o Howard Wolberton, P.O. Box 1126, East Orange, NJ 07019), Remember That Song (Box 3006, Glendale, AZ 85311), and The Sheet Music Exchange (P.O. Box 69, Quicksburg, VA 22847). The quality of the clubs varies; try them all until you find the one best suited to your needs.

One final point is worth mentioning. When a piece of sheet music is framed, its value perspective may change. No longer is it viewed solely as a collectible. It now has the added value inherent in a decorator accent item. Much of the common sheet music with decorative covers is marketed in this manner. Collectors should value the sheet as though it were outside the frame, add their estimate of the framing cost, and purchase only when the two values coincide. Any value above this figure is purely decorative and speculative. This is a good general rule to remember for any framed object.

I Have an Old Typewriter . . .

DID you ever fall in love with your typewriter? Most people who use one do. If you cut your typing teeth on an electric IBM Executive model from the late 1950s, you cannot look at one of those now-archaic mechanical monsters without strong feelings of nostalgia or heart palpitations. Typewriters simply become part of your life.

Further, mechanical typewriters tended to develop a personality all their own. Don't tell me this didn't happen. Over the past decades I owned several electric and portable typewriters that definitely had minds of their own. They certainly did not always type what I intended.

Each month I receive several letters from readers who want to know the value of an old typewriter that they found in their attic or office storage. Two recent requests inquired about a Corona portable with patent dates of 1913 and 1917 and an Underwood from the 1920s. Unfortunately, the answer in almost every case for machines dating after World War I is that they have little or no value to collectors at the moment.

One of the premier typewriter collectors in America is Richard B. Dickerson (620 South Sierra Bonita, Pasadena, CA 91106). His simple rule is that if a typewriter has four rows of keys, single shift, and front stroke, its value is minimal, except in rare cases. This eliminates most typewriters made in the post–World War I period.

According to Dickerson, a serious typewriter collection contains twenty-five to fifty machines and a major collection about a hundred machines. The number of serious and major typewriter collectors in the United States is extremely small, a closely knit group of approximately thirty to forty individuals. They all know each other, keeping in touch through private correspondence and the *ETCetera*, the quarterly newsletter of the Early Typewriter Collectors Association (11433 Rochester Avenue, #303, Los Angeles, CA 90025).

They also control prices to some extent. Since the number of collectors is small, the number of potential buyers for any old machine also is small. Finding two buyers that will compete against each other and force the price to its highest level is almost impossible.

Several general antiques and collectibles price guides have run prices for some of the pre-1920 machines. Since the prices are submitted to them by collectors, questions must be raised about their accuracy. Dickerson noted a recent price guide that showed a Coffman Pocket patent typewriter at $125. There are only three examples of this typewriter known. A serious or major collector would pay five times this price or more for a model in very good working condition. Was the person who prepared the list manipulating the price information in hopes of having someone offer him one of these typewriters at this much lower price?

Success is a detriment to a typewriter's collectibility. Successful machines were made in vast numbers and glut the limited buyer's market. The serious and major collectors cherish the failures, those typewriters that enjoyed limited production. Most serious and major collectors know specifically how many of each model are known. Dickerson was thrilled when a response to his want ad in a trade paper brought him a brass, portable automatic from the years 1887 to 1891.

His purchase increased the number of known examples from three to four.

Finding information about early typewriters is difficult. Michael H. Adler's *The Writing Machine* (Allen & Unwin, 1973), the best book in English, is out of print. *Collector's Guide to Antique Typewriters,* edited by Dan Post and available from Post-Era Books, is a reprint of "A Condensed History of the Writing Machine" which appeared in the October 1923 issue of *Typewriter Topics, the International Business Equipment Magazine.* It is loaded with historical data but contains no information about pricing.

Dickerson recommended reading a recent Panasonic promotional booklet edited by Frank T. Masi entitled "The Typewriter Legend." A copy can be obtained by writing to the Panasonic Consumer Affairs Division, 1 Panasonic Way, Secaucus, NJ 07094. There is a pamphlet dealing with the early history of IBM typewriters entitled "IBM: Yesterday and Today." Its IBM reference number is G520–3140–2 and the cost is $4.70, in case you want to order a copy from the company.

Actually, the most avid collectors of typewriters are not found in the United States but in Europe. The Europeans, especially the Germans, have organized several collectors' clubs, one of which covers the entire field of office machines. Ernst Martin's *Die Schreibmachine* is the masterwork on typewriters. European collectors have great difficulty finding early machines since most were destroyed during the wars, when they were melted down as scrap. European collectors consider the Americans quite fortunate since the possibility of locating early machines in attics, closets, and basements is still possible.

According to Dickerson, the current market for pre-1920 typewriters is soft. I agree. In light of this, is the best advice I can give those who own old typewriters from the 1920s and later to junk them? The realist in me has to answer yes. Sell them for scrap; use them for boat anchors. But the collector inside me says: Wait a minute. Someday, sometime, somebody will start collecting them.

A few typewriters from the later period are beginning to attract collectors. An Underwood Number #1 now is in the $50 to $75 range. How do you know you have a Number #1? Quite simple, it has no number. The company didn't think about numbering its typewriters until they developed the second model. The price for the Underwood Number #1 is the exception, not the rule.

The workhorse Remington portable of the 1920s, considered to be the most dependable of the portable typewriters, can be found at flea markets and shops throughout the United States in the $12 to $15 range. Several repair companies still stock parts for its repair. In truth, any price for a post-1920 machine over $15 should be questioned by any potential collector. I would gladly buy an old "Allen," invented by Richard Uhlig and made in Allentown, Pennsylvania, in working order at that price.

I recently discovered "The Typewriter Trader," a computer-compiled newsletter that publishes notices from individuals who wish to buy, sell, or trade antique typewriters. You may obtain a copy by sending a self-addressed, stamped envelope to: The Typewriter Trader, 11433 Rochester Avenue, #303, Los Angeles, CA 90025. There is no regular publication schedule since the newsletter is updated daily.

"Working-place antiques" offer a wonderful opportunity for a new collector with vision and a place to store them. Unfortunately, they have attracted little attention because the high-style collectors claim that working-place antiques have little or no aesthetic value. Well, several museums and individuals have discovered that vacuum cleaners and irons from the twentieth century are aesthetically designed. Why not examine the design of office products, such as typewriters, as well? The trained eye will see the elegance and aesthetics exhibited by some of the better-designed machines.

Will the same be true for computers someday? Dickerson feels that the computer has "zero charm" and will never be able to be compared to the elegance of some of the old typewriters. Computer companies arise. Opportunity knocks. Design us an incredible sexy, aesthetic computer. Make Dickerson eat his words. Give us an art museum masterpiece of the future.

It's Time for Another World's Fair

AMERICANS are conditioned to accept change as a key element in their lifestyle. Manufacturers rely on planned obsolescence to create a steady demand for their products. The trash crisis of the late 1980s confirms our commitment to living in a throwaway society. What this signifies is that most Americans have a short attention span.

This attitude influences the collectibles field. The collectibles market is cyclical. Collecting fads and phases cause continual price fluctuations in collectibles categories as they become hot or cool off. Few categories can sustain a high degree of collecting enthusiasm lasting a decade or longer. But almost every category becomes a "hot" collectible once every twenty-five years, and some more frequently.

One thing that can trigger renewed interest in collecting categories is a regular recurring event. Olympic collectibles and presidential campaign material provide two examples. Although presidential political collectibles have a solid collector base, the magazine, newspaper, radio and television hype surrounding each presidential campaign focuses on past elections for background stories and comparison pieces. During the six months prior to the November, 1988, presidential election, a wealth of articles on political campaign material appeared in trade papers and the popular media. If you kept your eyes open, you saw that I was right.

Anniversaries of events also trigger collecting interest. Collectibles associated with Halley's comet enjoyed great popularity a few years ago. Now they have disappeared—no buyers. Patriotic collectibles, such as Uncle Sam material, that were strong during the Bicentennial craze have suffered a similar fate.

Let's not dwell on the past. There are some key anniversaries that promise to create a wave of collecting enthusiasm coupled with an almost certain rise in prices. The fiftieth anniversary of World War II will be 1991 to 1995. Remember the collecting craze for Civil War material between 1960 and 1965. It might be insignificant when compared to the projected World War II craze.

For now I want to focus on 1993—not in relationship to a fifty-year-old event, but to one that occurred one hundred years ago: The Columbian Exposition, *a.k.a.* the 1893 Chicago World's Fair. Collecting interest in the Columbian Exposition was very strong in the late 1960s when the fair celebrated its seventy-fifth anniversary. By the mid-1980s a few diehard collectors kept the focus alive, but the sale and trading of Columbian Exposition material was minimal. The 1876 Centennial Exposition in Philadelphia was the hot fair.

Since nostalgia plays a big part in collectible collecting, I thought Columbian Exposition material would simply become one more esoteric category on the fringe of the collectibles market. After all, almost all the individuals and participants associated with the fair had died. The stoneware mug that grandfather Rinker acquiring during his 1893 visit to Chicago is one of my few links to him: He died in 1941, before my birth.

The revival of interest in the 1893 Chicago World's Fair as its centennial approaches clearly demonstrates the power of anniversaries to renew collecting trends and lead to a rapid rise in prices for objects in that collecting category. A recent discussion with Michael Pender, editor of *Fair News*, and Al Raymond (Raymond's Antiques, P.O. Box 509, Richfield Springs, NY 13439), a leading dealer in world's fair material, confirmed this trend. Both named memorabilia from the 1893 Columbian Exposition as the hottest among the specialized collector. Al called particular attention to material that was specifically exhibited at the fair as a highly desired item.

Another world's fair benefitting from the anniversary effect is the 1939 New York World's Fair. Pender and Raymond named this as the second hottest fair. I'm not surprised. Prices of 1939 New York World's Fair material have doubled, tripled, and even quadrupled in many cases during the past year.

The collecting interest in objects associated with the modernist movement of the early 1930s through 1950 also is fueling the increased prices for 1939 New York World's Fair material. The fair heralded the "steamlined" age. Many of the design elements that govern our household and office environment were completed or under development during the late 1930s. The impact of the 1939 New York World's Fair on the public was major.

Since so many of the souvenirs and other memorabilia of the 1939 New York World's Fair exhibit a modernistic design, the world's fair collector is in direct competition with the period or theme collector. The latter seem very willing to outbid the fair collector in almost every instance. It also means that prices are much higher than they ought to be. When the craze for modernistic collecting ends, it is questionable how many of these high prices will be sustained. Meanwhile, the world's fair collectors are (1) simply waiting until they can gain control of their own market again and (2) remembering that most material was made in hundreds of thousands, so there remains a wealth of undiscovered items in attics, basements, closets, and drawers. As high prices for 1939 New York World's Fair material are reported, the market will be flooded with more and more goods, thus reducing the scarcity level of many pieces and causing the base sticker price on many objects to drop.

I have stressed the modernistic, steamlined aspect of the 1939 New York World's Fair. However, the fair also had a strong element of traditionalism, especially in the American art displayed in the Gallery of American Art Today. Apollo Books (5 Schoolhouse Lane, Poughkeepsie, NY 12603) recently reprinted *American Art Today*, the catalog from the 1939 New York World's Fair exhibition. Regional juries of American artists and museum directors screened more than 25,000 entries to select the 1,200 works that were exhibited. Although the Surrealists and Abstractions were represented, I was struck by the large number of traditional works. The book is a wonderful contrast to the surface image of the fair. It also demonstrates that perhaps the industrial designers of the late 1930s were more style- and trend-conscious than the art community.

Collectors of world's fair and exposition material are fortunate to have two organizations that focus on their specialty: the Expo Collectors-Historians Organization (ECHO) (1436 Killarney Avenue, Los Angeles, CA 90065) and World Fair Collectors Society (P.O. Box 20806, Sarasota, FL 34238). Members of the latter group receive *Fair News* as part of their membership. *World's Fair* (P.O. Box 339, Corte Madera, CA 94925), published quarterly, is a perfect blend of historical articles, information about current and coming fairs and trade shows, and classified ads. A one year subscription costs $24.

Fairs and expositions after 1939 currently enjoy a minimum of collector interest. Hence, they offer an excellent opportunity to the collector on a limited budget. As late as 1986 you could still buy souvenirs of the 1962 Century 21 Seattle fair at the original 1962 prices. The surplus of unsold material from the fair was large.

I did ask Mike Pender if material from the more recent fairs was being hoarded by collectors. He told me he has not found evidence of this. In fact, he said there is a scarcity of material for the 1958 Universal Brussels exposition.

There are several pre-1939 fairs that also offer some real collecting opportunities, not the least of which is the 1933 Century of Progress in Chicago. Al Raymond called my attention to a miniature child's wagon that is priced in the $75 to $90 range. It is quite rare, but the price is low because of minimum collector interest. Two other possibilities are the 1901 Pan-American Exposition in Buffalo and the 1904 Louisiana Purchase Exposition in St. Louis.

Finally, keep in mind the power of key anniversaries to create a rise in prices in select collectible categories. Anticipating these events may allow you to acquire a few goodies before prices escalate.

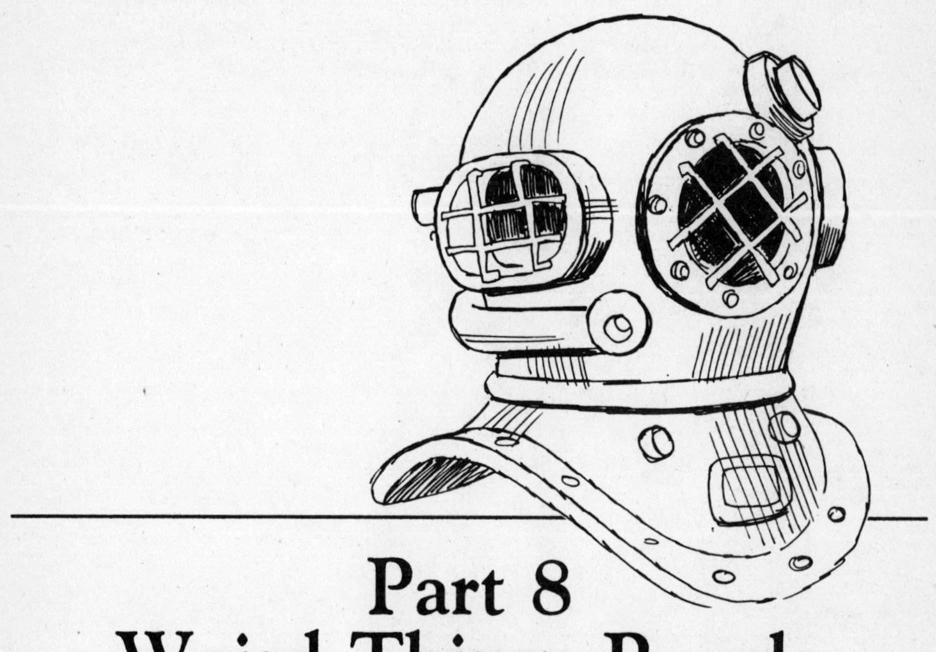

Part 8
Weird Things People Collect

Barf . . .

DURING a flight on US Air, the plane in which I was riding suddenly dropped 3,000 feet, lost pressure in the cabin, causing the oxygen masks to drop, and went into a dive reminiscent of a Navy corsair supporting John Wayne and the Marines in a World War II movie. Each stewardess dived for the nearest available spare seat, more concerned with attaching their own oxygen mask than for the welfare of their passengers. Devoid of any comforting presence, my thoughts alternated between quickly writing my last will and testament (I plan to see my attorney tomorrow) or reaching for the air sickness bag. I chose the latter.

If the term "air sickness" or "motion discomfort" bag is unfamiliar, perhaps you will recognize it by its more common name, "barf" bag.

When we reached 10,000 feet, the cabin repressurized. A crisis was averted. I had to pry my sweaty hand loose from a crumpled air sickness bag. As I straightened the bag out, I noticed that it did not contain any US Air identification – no logo, no name, no nothing. It was a generic bag, a type and design that could be used by any airline. The bag had the following message in English, French, and Spanish in white letters on a red ground: "FOR MOTION DISCOMFORT/CLOSE BY FOLDING TOWARD YOU/CLAMP SHUT WITH THE TABS/CALL CABIN ATTENDANT FOR DISPOSAL." A quick tour of the cabin revealed that US Air's generic air sickness bags also came in blue and gray tones, in addition to the red one in the seat pocket in front of me.

If you have followed my columns, you already know what is coming next. Yes, I have a "barf" bag collection. It started a little over a year ago, when "Krissy" Verderosa, a friend's daughter, was making a trip to Florida on Peoples' Airline. Rumors abounded that Peoples' was about to go out of business, so I asked Krissy to pick up any items that she could find that had the airline's logo on them. She brought me a Peoples' "barf" bag.

From this small seed, a collection grew. Thus far, I have air sickness bags that have a name, logo, or both of an airline on them from British Airways, Delta Air Lines, Eastern, and Mexicana. The British Airways bag is the largest, almost double the capacity of any other airlines' bag. I do not know the significance of this. You draw your own conclusions. Eastern has two sizes of bags, one slightly bigger than the other. Why remains a mystery.

I have done some research on "barf" bags to see if I could determine the pièce de résistance, the ultimate unit. I think I found a candidate. In the early 1960s Eastern Airlines apparently had an air sickness bag that served a double purpose. If you did not throw up in it, you could use it to mail your camera film to Kodak for processing. It would take a lot to top this.

"Barf" bags are only one part of my bag collection, ranging in scope from paper supermarket bags to plastic department store bags. Why save bags? If you stop and think about it, it makes sense. During the 1976 Olympic games in Los Angeles, McDonald's issued a number of premiums with the Olympic logo on them. Hundreds, if not thousands, probably saved the three-dimensional items. How many saved the bag with the logo design on it? When Olympic collectibles, fast food collectibles, and bag collectibles hit it big, I am going to own a premium piece.

As much as I oppose the concept, rarity plays a critical factor in the pricing of collectibles. When I think about a collecting category, I constantly ask the question, What is most likely to be thrown out? When I identify such objects, chances are that one or more examples end up in my collection.

We take bags for granted. We assume they are plain; we assume we should throw them out or use them for garbage. When was the last time you really looked at a bag?

Stores and other businesses have long viewed the bag as a valid advertising vehicle. Check out the shoppers at your local mall. As they walk around carrying their purchases, they are traveling billboards for the store in which they bought their first or second item.

The more you look at bags, the less neutral they become. You begin to recognize that most bag decoration has a strong design element. The more you investigate, the more you realize that a bag that merely touts a store or business's logo is actually a rather ordinary bag. "Real" bags have vivid, exciting, and appealing designs.

A bag can be both functional and a work of art. No one understands this more than the Europeans. Their plastic shopping bags are fantastic. Stores and businesses actually compete for the most trendy, eye-catching design.

Karin Bartl, Raimund Bartl, and Volkmar Schnöke's *Plastiktüten: Kunst zum Tragen* (Hannover: Fackelträger-Verlag, 1986) is the first serious study of the plastic bag as an art form. It is printed in German, but it is worth buying for the pictures alone. The colored photographs of plastic bags illustrate everything from the enormous power of a company logo to the responsiveness of designers to fashion trends. The book details the manufacturing method of the modern plastic bag and provides a detailed classification system for plastic bag types. An English edition is needed.

Bag collectors collect in a vacuum. They are not organized. But the bubble-gum and candy-wrapper collectors, close cousins, are. Information can be obtained by writing *The Wrapper*, c/o Les Davis, 1903 Ronzheimer Avenue, St. Charles, IL 60174.

Again, youthful stupidity stares me in the face. As I chewed pack after pack of bubble gum to build my "Hopalong Cassidy" bubble-gum card collection, I tossed the wrappers in the trash without giving them a second thought. Almost every youngster saved bubble-gum cards; almost no one saved the wrapper. Today I buy "Hopalong Cassidy" bubble-gum cards in the 50¢ to $2 each range. If I get lucky and find the wrapper, it probably will cost me well over $50. I paid $30 for the Hoppy candy-bar wrapper in my collection.

I wish I could tell you that I learned from my youthful mistake and now have the world's largest bubble-gum and candy-wrapper collection. Alas, I do not. I have saved a few, but I have never made it a priority. You see, when things are so cheap and easy to save, it hardly seems worth the effort.

Do You Know What Day It Is Today?

IT'S January 14, 1987, as I sit and write this column. I wonder what day it is? No, I know it's Wednesday. What I am thinking is what person, group, event, or other occurrence has been designated for celebration on this momentous day in my life? Just as certain as the sun rises each morning is the reality that some legislative body, religion, or organization has designated this day to honor some special cause or individual.

What about January 14? Well, it marks the birth of Benedict Arnold in 1741, William Whipple (signer of the Declaration of Independence) in 1730, and Albert Schweitzer in 1875. The day is Vinegrower's Day in Bulgaria, the beginning of the Aspen-Snowmass (Company) winter carnival, the Austin Texas Sport Motor cycle show, the beginning of the Bob Hope Chrysler Classic Golf Tournament in California, and the National Western Stock Show in Denver. The moon officially enters its full moon phase on this date.

Historically, January 14 is the anniversary of the ratification of the Treaty of Paris in 1794, the launching of Soyuz 4 in 1969, and the day before filing your quarterly estimated Federal Income Tax payment.

We must extend a debt of gratitude, tongue in check, to William and Helen Chase, whose *Chase's Annual Events: Thirteenth Annual Edition* (Contemporary Books, 1986) provided me with the above information.

Think about it. All these special events associated with their special days must generate collectibles. Here's a collecting category that no one is exploring. The possibilities are endless.

I mean, really, should the true collector rest content having collectibles only associated with the traditional holidays such as Christmas, New Year's, Valentine Day's, Easter, Mother's Day, Father's Day, Fourth of July, Halloween, and Thanksgiving? It's time to expand our horizons.

The conspiracy between the candy, card, floral, and gift industry to make us part with our money in the name of love, friendship, or keep-ups-manship already has resulted in several new "important dates," such as Professional Secretaries' Day (April 22), Grandparents' Day (September 13), and Boss's Day (October 16). Personally I attach special significance to the fact that Mother-in-Law's Day occurs just six days before Halloween. Someone has a sense of humor!

The latest of the "important dates," as headlined in the Hallmark calendar book, is Sweetest Day, scheduled for Saturday, October 17. What is Sweetest Day? I never heard of it, a fact to which my staff nods their heads in agreement without question. Did you?

To get the word direct from the horse's mouth so to speak, I called John Sanders from Michigan, a member of the Sweetest Day Committee. His secretary, who informed me that she has been the recipient of several Sweetest Day gifts in the past, explained that the origins of the day are attributed to Herbert Birch Kingston of Cleveland, Ohio, who, some sixty years ago, delivered gifts to the poor one day each fall. Eventually the day grew to be one of "remembrance and special feeling for others."

In exploring the types of gifts that are appropriate for Sweetest Day, I found that candy, cards, flowers, and gifts fit the bill. "It sounds like Valentine's Day in the fall," I said to Mr. Sanders's secretary. "Bingo," was her reply.

As I was about to hang up from my call, I thought to ask what John Sanders does for a living. Take a guess. He is with Fred Sanders of Highland Park, Michigan, a candy manufacturer whose company has been in business for over one hundred and eleven years. Thank you, Hallmark, and your calendar. You scratch my back and I'll scratch yours.

When I was in grade school, I looked forward to February. If the dates fell right, two vacation days were granted—one for Lincoln's birthday and one for Washington's birthday. I never asked for a four-day Presidents' Day weekend. I liked the unexpected treat of a day off in the middle of the week. It was like having the benefits of staying home sick without really being sick.

Further, the objects available for the celebration of President's Day do not begin to rival the great display items associated with the separate celebrations for Lincoln's and Washington's birthday during my youth. Oh, the Bicentennial and Statue of Liberty celebrations have temporarily brought back the nation's love of red, white, and blue and witnessed the reappearance of a few hatchets and cherry trees. But, if I am correct, the end is already in sight.

Collecting holiday material began with the Valentine collectors. The late 1970s and early 1980s saw the arrival of the Christmas collectors. At the moment, the hottest holiday is Halloween. Holiday collectibles now are an entrenched part of our collecting mania.

The next big collecting craze should center on Easter, with St. Patrick's Day, the Fourth of July, and Thanksgiving not too far behind. Collectors simply have not yet exhausted the very traditional holidays, although I doubt if Memorial Day or Labor Day material will ever generate too much enthusiasm.

But no real collector forgets that the rarest, most expensive objects in his collecting field are the earliest items. Be alert for the new "important days" as they occur. Stash away a few items. Amaze your grandchild at the gullibility of individuals in the 1980s. Rest assured, they will find some collector in 2050 to whom they can sell the material.

On a final note, there is always a spoilsport. He is Harold Fullman Coffin, a newspaper man, who created in 1973 the famous unholiday, National Nothing Day. Coffin wanted one day a year when there was nothing to celebrate. He did not bother to get a Presidential Proclamation or have his day listed in *Chase's Annual Events*. While Coffin and his advocates may not recognize the potential inherent in National Nothing Day, we collectors must. Arise! "Let's all get out there and do something for Nothing."

Oil of Mink and Me

DURING a visit to the Hyatt Hotel in Indianapolis, I was confronted by one of the great dilemmas of modern times. Should I use the Swiss Spa Bath Gelee with Oil of Mink, French Formula Shampoo with Oil of Mink, Soft Awakening Hand & Body Moisturizer with Oil of Mink, French Formula Creme Hair Conditioner with Oil of Mink, a combination, or all of them? It is unreasonable to force a person to make this type of decision at 7:00 a.m.

American consumers are rapidly being caught up in the great hotel giveaway sweepstakes. In addition to the above-mentioned items, the large black plastic rectangle that consumed approximately one-third of the vanity in the bathroom at the Hyatt contained a box of French Milled Luxury Personal Soap, Glycerine Soap, French Milled Luxury Bath Soap, a shower cap, a bottle of talc, a shoehorn, and a sachet. The sink took up another third of the vanity area. The two glasses, ashtray, and pack of matches consumed additional space. I hardly had a place for my shaving kit.

Like all individuals with a strong sense of curiosity, I decided to see what would happen if I took everything off the black plastic rectangle and put it in a drawer. Like magic, another set of material appeared. As quickly as I hid them, someone replaced them. I wondered if my suitcase would be big enough to get them all home.

What womb was the birthplace of this vast array of endless goodies? Careful investigation revealed it to be a large rectangular metal cart that contained some practical things as well, such as towels and toilet paper.

The person who designed the Indianapolis Hyatt was certainly aware of the need to provide space for the free giveaways. I wish he would have given as much thought to providing space for the spare roll of toilet paper. Alas, there was no storage space under the sink. The spare roll was outside the bathroom on the top shelf of the closet, not a convenient location.

Prior to the late 1970s the biggest souvenir from a hotel stay was a picture postcard, a pen, a bar of soap, or a shoe-horn. Hotels got angry if you swiped the towels or the ashtrays.

My collection includes a shoe-box filled with hotel collectibles from past and present. I have Palmolive soap from the Ambassador Hotel in Washington, D.C., the Statler Hotels, and the Hotel Jermyn in Scranton, Pennsylvania, Ivory soap from the Ambassador in Los Angeles and the Statler system, Colgate's Floating Soap from the Abraham Lincoln in Reading, Pennsylvania, and Camay from the Virginia Dare Hotel in Elizabeth City, North Carolina.

Most of these examples were given to me by Sonny Moore, my father-in-law and fellow saver. We have a contest going. We pass along to one another things that simply are too neat to throw out. He gave me a collection of hotel soaps from the 1930s and 1940s that he scrounged from his brother before they hit the trash can, and I blessed him with a pair of shellacked piranha that were in the trash box at an estate I was appraising. I might point out that my generosity to my father-in-law is not always greeted with the same enthusiasm by my mother-in-law. *[Note: Since writing this column, Sonny Moore died. I miss him both as a source of supply and a friend.]*

Collectors need to develop some type of formula for selling or swapping this wealth of hotel giveaways with which we are being afflicted. Is a Hyatt French Formula Shampoo with Oil of Mink equal to a Hotel du Pont Balanced Protein Shampoo, or should the trade be two for one? Do three Gilchrist & Soames shower caps equal one Mark Hopkins Inter-Continental soap?

The same critical decisions that face the Avon collectors and limited edition whiskey bottle collectors now face the hotel giveaway collectors. Is the bottle of Hyatt Swiss Bath Gelee with Oil of Mink worth as much if it is empty? My wife would like this to be the case, since she really likes many of the formulas and is pressing me to allow her to use the small treasure trove of shampoo, conditioner, and moisturizer that I have accumulated. I have not decided as yet.

Just one note of caution. For some reason that I simply cannot understand, our modern hotels do not anticipate that its guests might wish to save and take home the goodies that they provide. The person who designed the plastic bottles for the Hyatt chain never gave any thought to air travel. I know. I have over ten dollars in cleaning bills for the removal of quantities of shampoo, conditioner, and moisturizer with oil of mink from my pants and coats.

But don't worry. I'm prepared for next time. I have already put a few Baggies in my suitcase to hold the stuff I'm going to save during my next trip.

Hidden Treasures

I have been drinking Red Rose tea for over five years, in part because I like its flavor and in part because of the Wade porcelain animal miniatures that are offered as premiums. The other morning I was opening a new box, excited about the prospect of acquiring either a langur, pine martin, tiger, or beaver — the four animals I am missing from the current wild animal series of fifteen different miniatures. Alas, I obtained another gorilla.

As I placed the gorilla among my assortment of duplicate animals, I suddenly realized what I was doing to myself. I had nine duplicates. Nine duplicates! Each represents a hundred cups of tea that I drank for the privilege of buying another box of tea in hopes that I might someday, through sheer luck, complete my set of figures.

I hate hidden treasures when they are in series. They are unfair to collectors. They constitute a form of cruel and unusual punishment that should be made illegal for manufacturers and others to use.

When I was younger, collecting things in series was much easier. Being a Hopalong Cassidy fan, I consumed an inordinate amount of Bond bread, primarily to get the Hopalong Cassidy end flaps. Pasted on a master sheet, these end flaps told a story. Luck had nothing to do with completing your set. You saw the flap before you bought it. All you had to do was get a loaf with an end flap you did not have.

The same held true for cereal boxes. If the box had a cutout mask on the back, whether a "Lone Ranger" character or someone from the "Howdy Doody" show, you could see what you were buying before you ate the cereal. While you may have had to go to more than one store until you found the mask you needed for your set, at least you did not have to eat an extra box of the stuff.

The same held true for cereal and radio premiums. You sent in so many labels and some postage money and received the object of your heart's desire, possibly a "Captain Midnight" decoder or "Orphan Annie" dog whistle. The way was clear. You knew what you had to consume in order to obtain the final prize. No more, no less—just the right amount.

Of course, the principal problem area was bubble gum. Random luck was at work. But the smart youngster realized that a full box of gum cards almost always contained a full set of the cards. If you bought the gum by the box instead of the pack, you put your set together rather quickly. I never did understand how the card companies kept track of all this, but I always said a silent prayer at night for the individuals who kept the system functioning.

What about Cracker Jacks prizes? Surely, they were random luck. Actually, the prizes posed no problem. The makers of Cracker Jacks, in their infinite wisdom, kept the number of series prizes to a minimum. There was the train with its engine and assorted cars. But in reality, each prize stood on its own.

Hidden treasures frustrate me. I do not have the patience to allow them to work their mysterious ways, eventually ensuring me a complete collection of Wade miniatures, gum cards, or whatever else I am collecting. When I want to build a collection, I want to do it immediately, get it done, and move on to something else.

Frequently, I am baffled by the hidden treasures of the past because I find something numbered "19" or "27" and cannot locate a list of the objects in the series. Collectors of comic, movie, baseball, television/radio, and western series buttons have found this problem most ably resolved in *Buttons in Sets* by Marshall N. Levin and Theodore L. Hake (Hake's Americana and Collectibles, P.O. Box 1444, York, PA 17405). But all too often, the list of the components of the hidden treasure series has been lost.

Baseball card collectors have it made. Realizing that most collectors only tolerated the bubble gum to get at the cards, Topps and other manufacturers finally decided to issue full boxed sets of the cards without wrappers or bubble gum. For a very modest price, the collector can have a full set of the cards immediately. It makes sense to me.

When Red Rose ended its original wild animal miniature series, they allowed individuals to purchase the animals they needed to complete their set. The price was 50¢ per animal, or $7.50 for a complete set. I wanted to cry. Why did I drink all that Red Rose tea? I should have waited. Did I learn my lesson? Certainly not.

As you already know, I am hard at work collecting the new series. Frustration remains a vital part in all of this. Frankly, I suspect that Redco Foods, distributors of Red Rose, only packages one animal at a time. Whenever my wife buys two boxes at the same time at the same store, I always get a duplicate. This is not random luck. It certainly is not explained on the box.

To overcome the possibility of getting duplicates when I need more than one box of tea, I have my wife go to two separate stores. I reason that perhaps one store uses a different supplier who is not as quick in selling his stock as the supplier of the second store. Shopping at the second store enhances my chance of getting two different animals from two different shipments from Redco Foods. It makes sense to me. My wife of course has her own opinion about this logic.

All Toilet Paper Is Not Created Equal

IF you have traveled abroad or used an outhouse, you are aware of one basic truth—all toilet paper is not created equal. What a perfect excuse to collect it.

On the surface, collecting toilet paper need not be an expensive hobby. Selected pilfering from public restrooms and friends' bathrooms will provide enough examples to begin a collection. Of course, if you travel abroad to obtain examples, the costs increase considerably. However, I discovered that once my friends found out that I have a toilet paper collection, their desire to enhance my collection with their personal contributions caused examples to simply roll in.

I became aware of the collectible potential of toilet paper in the late 1970s when I learned about a woman who was appearing on the Womens' Club lecture circuit talking about the wide assortment of toilet paper that she encountered during her travels. She charged a fee for her presentation and did not seem to lack bookings. She obviously was cleaning up.

After resisting the urge to follow suit for almost a decade, I simply gave up and began my own toilet paper collection. My initial beginnings were modest. I wrote to several German friends and asked them to send me some examples of German toilet paper. Udo, my friend in Hamburg, outdid himself. Among the examples he sent was toilet paper from the German railroad.

A close examination of the light gray textured paper revealed that each sheet was stamped "Deutsche Bundesbahn." This says something about a nation's character. The German railroad administration is so concerned about a roll of toilet paper that they find it necessary to stamp their name on every sheet so that if someone takes some and uses it outside a train bathroom, the user is pointedly reminded that they are, in essence, using stolen property.

The ridiculousness of the German railroad administration is surpassed by the English government. When you use the public restrooms in museums throughout England, you quickly notice that each sheet of toilet paper is marked "Official Government Property." What a subtle way to recognize that your tax dollars are at work.

The U.S. military issued its field troops camouflage toilet paper. It seems the Viet Cong followed mounds of used white stuff to track our troop movements during the Vietnam War. What happened to the good old collapsible GI shovel? The use of camouflage toilet paper has been discontinued. It seems the dyes had a stinging effect on GI posteriors.

Since toilet paper collecting is in its infancy, now is an excellent time to create rules concerning how to accumulate this important new collectible. For example, how many sheets are necessary to have a valid example? Ideally, I suggest four to six; but a minimum of two, one to keep in mint condition and the other to record the time and place of acquisition, will do in a pinch.

Do you collect single sheets or the entire roll? This is a tough one. I started out by collecting sheets. Then I began thinking about the potential value of wrappers and added them to my collection. Since I had gone that far, I figured why not save the entire roll. When I realized that some rolls were packaged in units of four to six, I was forced to save the entire package. My collection, which originally was meant to be confined to a shirt box, now occupies several large boxes.

Toilet paper collecting provides an engaging topic for cocktail parties and other social gatherings. Everyone has a toilet paper story to tell. I remember the time I had to use the facilities in the basement of the Moravian Archives in Herrnhut, East Germany. The nature of the call required that I immediately locate a toilet with no regard to the toilet paper status. Later examination revealed no toilet paper, but rather an old railroad time-schedule booklet with some of the pages torn out. As I tore a sheet loose, the ink on the paper came off on my fingers. You can imagine the rest. I should have saved an example, but I wasn't thinking of toilet paper collecting at the time.

I think everyone should be required to use a farm or camp outhouse at some point in their lives. The stories of corn-cobs and Sears catalogs are true. I know. I remember the concern expressed by my rural relatives when Sears switched to glossy paper stock. I have a number of old catalogs in my collection.

As my toilet paper collection grew, I become fascinated with the composition and variety of designs and patterns of toilet paper. When I first visited Germany in the late 1960s, their extremely coarse gray toilet paper had the quality of sandpaper. In 1987 I found that German toilet paper tastes now matched the Americans' desire for soft, almost tissue-like paper. The significance of this shift and what it says about the development of the German character should not be overlooked.

As with all my collections, I have some favorite examples, among which are a half-roll of toilet paper that a friend brought me from England that has a surface texture equivalent to wax paper and a German aluminum foil package that contains toilet paper moistened and perfumed to act and smell like a wash and dry. I have a special box in which I put translucent examples, those you can see through when held up to the light. Their use gives real meaning to the phrase "doubling up."

Thus far I have been unsuccessful in locating other serious toilet paper collectors. They exist; there are collectors for everything. If I can locate them, I would be glad to discuss swapping duplicates.

Meanwhile, you can help. The next time your travels in the USA or abroad bring you into contact with the unusual during a period of daily meditation, save a few examples and send them to me. Is there the making of a future museum collection here? Time will tell.

Part 9
The Future

Two Hundred Dollars and a Closet (1987)

IT'S Christmas, the time of the year that generates more future collectibles than any other period. I should be happy. Instead, I find myself banging my head against the wall. Christmas, yuck! All I think about are the forty-five Christmas opportunities I wasted. Why, if I had only not played with my toys or let my children play with their toys, if I only had bought things and put them away, if . . . , if . . . , if . . . .

Well, it's never too late. This year is going to be different. This year I will spend some money, buy tomorrow's collectibles, find a safe place to store them for thirty years, and then reap my rewards in the early years of retirement.

My plan is simple. Beginning now I will spend two hundred dollars each year and buy the toys that I think will be collectible in thirty years. I can find space to store my new acquisitions in my clothes closet at the house. Besides, who really needs a big wardrobe?

Now I have the Christmas spirit. There is nothing an accumulator welcomes more than a buying spree. It's like a fix—the more goodies the better. Scrooge McDuck has his bin of gold coins in which to swim and play; I have my closets and other storage spaces.

My quest now resembles the search for the Holy Grail. The chain toy stores are pilgrimage stops. Have I properly prepared myself for this most noble of assignments? Undaunted, I proceed.

Since my children are now young adults, I had only spent a limited amount of time in toy stores during the past several years. I suffered shock when I saw the price of toys. Two hundred dollars hardly seemed adequate. If I was going to succeed, I would have to comparison shop and watch for bargains.

My first purchase was Barbie's Ferrari (Mattel, No. 3136) on sale at $15.97. I selected it over several other Barbie products because it was the most realistic-appearing of the Barbie material. The Barbie television studio and furniture is so abstract that it is meaningless. The Ferrari is great because it actually is a dual collectible. If the Barbie market weakens, it always will appeal to car collectors.

Another reason that I bought Barbie's Ferrari was for its great box. The picture of Barbie and the Ferrari is terrific. The quality of the box was an important consideration throughout my buying binge. I made several purchases just because of the boxes. Remember, collectors look for displayability, and the box is often a key factor.

One of the criteria that I imposed upon myself was to avoid buying any toys targeted for five-year-olds and under. Most adults remember the toys of their childhood and adolescence, not their infancy. This eliminated most of the Fisher-Price products. Yet I wanted to include something from this important and highly collectible toy manufacturer. After careful study, I bought a Fisher-Price Trike at $24.97. I rejected No. 2601, the purple-toned heart model, as too cute. Although I bought No. 2600, the trike I dubbed "Blue Lightning," the police cycle, No. 2603, probably would have served just as well.

Among my treasures, I wanted to include something related to a television character of the 1980s. I was tempted by several of the "Alf" dolls but finally settled on a battery-powered "Alf" toothbrush (Janex, No. 07025) at $12.99. Most individuals will save the dolls. How many will save the toothbrush? The toothbrush that I bought is a three-dimensional Alf. There is a less expensive model that has an Alf decal on the handle. Don't accept anything less than the top of the line.

My children played with Legos. I wanted to get something, but what? Then I remembered the large single box of Lego pieces now in storage at home. What good are the pieces without instructions? I tried to save my children's Lego boxes but was unsuccessful. The answer was obvious. Buy the *Lego Idea Book* for $1.99. In fact, I bought ten.

As I was walking from one aisle to another, I passed a display of lunch boxes. They probably should not be included on a Christmas list. But I noticed that almost every example was made from the same plastic mold with only a different stickum attached. The only two lithograph tin lunch boxes were Jim Henson's Muppet Babies (Thermos) at $4.89 and Secret Wars (Aladdin), featuring the Hulk, Captain America, and Spiderman, at $4.68. I added one example of each to my stash.

As I walked through the toy car section, I was surprised to see how few of the current car models had toy counterparts. I could find no preassembled BMWs or Hondas. It is a statement about the total lack of quality car design in the 1980s. Again, turning to an old reliable manufacturer, I bought a Tonka Road-Tough Pickup (No. 2200) at $10.99. There were several variations, including the Rock Hopper, Dirty Demo, and Road Runner. I chose the Fearsome 4 x 4.

Recently a lot of attention has focused on the strong militaristic aspect of many of the current crop of toys, especially since a number of California communities are banning the sale of realistic toy weapons. Since toy guns enjoy a strong collectors market, I felt an Uzi machine gun was appropriate. The choices were many. I could buy a motorized Uzi water machine gun (Larami, No. 9902–0) at $9.99, a Commando Uzi machine gun (Echo Toys Ltd, No. 81360) that makes a blasting sound and has smoke coming out of the barrel for $14.97, an Uzi (Esquire/Nichols, No. 7580) that shoots 250-roll caps per minute for $9.97, or a Rambo 9mm Automatic (Remco, No. 16010) on a 1:1 scale for $14.97. Every Rambo Uzi that I looked at was covered with dust, a fact that should tell Sylvester Stalone something. However, since I liked its packaging and it was a 1:1 scale, I opted for the Rambo Uzi.

Since I already have a large game collection, I thought it fitting to add some current examples. The two key factors were how well I thought the show would be remembered and the quality of the game box cover. I finally settled for The A Team Game (Parker Brothers, No. 0089) at $3.91, the Family Ties Game (Apple Street, No. 87–300) at $9.99, Miami Vice (Pepper Lane Industries, Division of Colorforms) at $7.91, Wheel of Fortune, second edition (Pressman, No. 5555), at $12.97, and Super Jock, Super Touch Basketball Game (Milton Bradley, No. 4795) at $13.97.

I love bargains. As I walked along the canyons created by the toy walls, I could not help but notice that many stores still had in inventory toys whose popularity waned several years ago. I quickly added to my collection the Tie Interceptor at $9.92, the Speeder Bike Vehicle at $2.93, and the Hoth Turret Defense Action Playset at $4.97 from the *Return of the Jedi* (Kenner). The 1980 The Legend of The Lone Ranger 10-Piece Rifle & Holster Set (Gabriel, No. 21716) at $17.97 was a similar addition.

I had less than ten dollars to go. I debated for a moment over the Michael Jackson Dress-Up Set (Colorforms, No. 2369) at $2.91, but opted for the Little Shopper Play Food (Nasta Industries Inc., No. 72849) for $5.96. The latter was not only a toy collectible but an advertising collectible as well.

The total was $199.95, not counting tax. The choices were difficult. There were many other toys I would have liked to include. Anyone want to lend me another two hundred dollars?

Two Hundred Dollars and a Closet (1988)

IT is time again for my annual safari into the toy jungle. Each year I plan to buy two hundred dollars worth of toys that I think will be both desirable and collectible thirty years from now. I will never play with them and will store them carefully. In 2018 I, or my successor, will compare their 1988 cost with their collectible market value then. It will be a good test of the investment potential of collectibles.

Having a four-year-old granddaughter makes the "I will never play with them" rule a major problem. This year's shopping trip was more expensive than I had planned. I had to buy two examples of several of the items so that my granddaughter and I could play with one of them. Ah, the sacrifices grandparents make.

My local toy jungle consists of a Kiddie City and Toys "R" US. However, my trek did detour as I wandered off-course to purchase a few goodies at other locations. Although I found that the 1988 toy market lacked the luster of past years, I still bagged a few trophies.

My first purchase was a still (non-mechanical-action) bank. Still banks are a blue chip collectible category. I bought HG Toys Ltd.'s Master of the Universe Skeletor bank ($3.97). I wanted to added several other still banks to my collection, but the remaining choices were pitiful. There was a Princess of Power She-Ra bank for the same price as the Skeletor bank, but I included this character in my collection by buying Janex Corporation's Princess Power She-Ra talking toothbrush ($15.97) that says "I eat food that's right and I brush my teeth morning, noon, and night." I used to own a car that talked, but traded it in for one that did not. I miss it. Can a talking toothbrush fill the void? Only time will tell.

I was startled this year by the lack of toys picturing major stars of television, movies, and music. The Pressman Wheel of Fortune game box design included a generic hostess, not a likeness of Vanna White. I prefer the real thing. The more I looked, the more I realized that star-endorsed products were disappearing. As a result, I focused much of my 1988 buying on items that had a definite star or character association.

I wanted to include an Alf collectible and selected Gordy International's No. 733 Alf Playset ($1.99) that included an 84" jump rope, three sticks of chalk, metal jacks, pocket yoyo, and high bounce ball. The packaging contained a great Alf picture. In the cartoon area, I was attracted by Dankin's Fun Farm Opus Holiday Hotel Doll ($9.99). A Centurion collectible was added with HG Toys Ltd.'s 36" Bop Bag ($3.97).

A visit to any toy jungle clearly demonstrates the dominance of the Saturday morning cartoon characters in toy merchandising. Personally, I prefer to wait until a show falls from grace and pick up its material on sale. As a result, I completely passed on all Dino-Rider and Transformer material. I did buy three Tonka Go-Bot figures—Major Mo, Night Ranger, and Crasher—for $1.49 each, reduced from $3.99.

I must confess that Teenage Mutant Ninja Turtles are a personal favorite, so I gave in to temptation and bought a few. Playmates' Turtle Blimp ($16.99) appeared to be a toy with limited survival, but great memory potential. Having one complete in thirty years will be a rarity. I also added two Random House Teenage Mutant Ninja Turtle puzzles at $1.99 each.

My other concession to Saturday morning television was Matchbox's Talking Pee Wee Herman Doll ($21.99). I rejected the other characters from the program in favor of Herman himself. I think he will be the best remembered in the long range.

Sports heroes are part of the American tradition. I resisted the small plastic figures that only resembled the individuals whose names appeared on the boxes. Besides, what guarantee do we have that they will eventually be in a hall of fame? I wanted pictures of real people with true hall of fame potential. Now included in my collection are Ohio Art's Michael Jordan Lil' Sport Hoops ($6.99), HG Toys Ltd.'s Dwight Gooden Automatic Pitch Up Set ($9.97) and Tyco's Gretzky 99 Hockey Puck Senior Model ($1.99). I rejected a "Dr. J" basketball item because I associate him more with the 1970s than I do with the 1980s.

When it comes to board games, I am cheap. I only buy games that are on sale. This year my purchases include Maruca Industries' Dallas: The Game of Empire Building Strategy ($9.99, reduced from $19.99), Pepper Lane Industries' Miami Vice: The Game ($7.91, reduced from $12.99), Parker Brothers' Willow ($4.91, reduced from $9.99), and TSR Inc.'s All My Children ($6.91, reduced from $15.97). I also added Remco's The Karate Kid Sato's Cannery that was on sale for $9.96. All the games have either a television or movie theme. However, I am a bit concerned that the television games are more adult than child related. Will anyone remember Miami Vice thirty years from now?

I was surprised and delighted to find an actual china set of child's dishes among the hoard of plastic sets. However, in addition to Summco International's sixteen-piece china tea set with a pastel flower transfer ($12.99), I also bought Worcester Toy Corporation's Campbell's Snack Time ($8.99), featuring the modern Campbell Kids. Time and time again I stress the multifaceted nature of collectibles. The broader the collecting interest in an object, the better the investment. The Campbell Snack Time has this broad appeal.

While in the kitchen area, I also purchased Multi-Toy Corporation's #9350 Burger King ($12.99), an actual life-size representation of a Burger King hamburger, and #9526 Kentucky Fried Chicken Lunch ($6.99). Fast-food collectibles continue to show increasing strength in the collectibles field, so adding a few items makes sense. Actually, I could just as well have chosen some of the Baskin Robbins, Dunkin' Donut, or Pizza Hut items. The key is that the items must look as realistic as possible.

Each year the fast-food chains offer many holiday premiums to entice customers. Each year I check them out. Each year I gain ten pounds. My 1988 favorites are clearly the MacDonald Muppet babies. I bought all three at $2.19 each. I also added an old standby, the 1988 Hess Truck and Racer at $6.95. Just remember to remove the battery for long-term storage. You do not want the battery to leak and ruin the toy.

Well, I only have $2.57 left to spend as I stand in front of the puzzle section. Actually, I had hoped to add several cartoon and television character puzzles to my collection this year. Now, I can afford only one. After careful deliberation, I will select Colorforms' Puzzleforms Michael Jackson thirty-piece puzzle with Colorform play pieces ($1.91, reduced from 3.79). The Disney, Smurf, Peanut, Captain America, and other characters will still be around next year and for years to come. I do not have the same faith in the durability of Michael Jackson. This may be one of the last chances to buy Michael Jackson collectibles. Take advantage of it.

Finally, it is worth mentioning some items that I did not buy and have no intention of buying. I thought the Definitely Dinosaurs material lacked quality, as well as any long-term collectibility. A lady who recognized me and realized that I was doing research for this column urged me not to consider My Little Pony Scented Toys. She said one came apart in her car trunk and produced a nauseating smell.

My final purchases totaled $199.34, not including sales tax. I am certain that I might have saved a few pennies here and there if I did some comparison shopping. Prices for the same item do vary from store to store. But, antiques and collectibles flea markets, shops, and shows beckon. I leave endurance toy shopping to the younger generation.

Old Collectors Never Die . . .

EVERY collector enjoys sharing his or her collection with other collectors. I am no exception. Inevitably, any visit includes a question that I wish would best be left unasked: "What's going to happen to all your stuff when you die?"

No true collector or accumulator ever thinks of dying. It is something that happens to other people, not to them. Collecting goes on forever and so do they. The bumper sticker on my car reads "Born to Collect," not "Dying to Sell."

Most collectors fall in love with their collection. Their collection is an extension of their family. It assumes a personality. It is alive, it grows. Selling one's collection is equivalent to selling one's children (something I know to be socially unacceptable, but contemplated once or twice during the raising of mine). The end result is that most collectors do not sell their collections during their lifetime.

Collections tend to be assembled by an individual. They rarely are family affairs. Most widows and children who inherit collections could care less. Their interest in maintaining the collection is minimal or nonexistent. In fact, the collection often represents the trips to Hawaii never taken or the new car that the family did not buy because the collector could not pass up the opportunity to add the one piece he truly needed to make his collection great. Unfortunately, this "one" piece has a bad habit of multiplying.

When I visit a fellow collector, I often see an object or two that I would like to add to my collection. I make it a firm practice to tell the collector that if he or she should ever wish to sell that object, I might be a willing buyer, so please give me a call. If you don't ask, how will the collector know you have an interest? I also make it a practice to make my remarks within hearing of the spouse. It may seem morbid, but when that collector dies, I want his spouse to remember that nice man that offered to buy some or all of the collection.

Individuals who inherit collections usually face two problems: (1) they are overwhelmed by the collection; and (2) they want to sell it as quickly as possible. Haste makes waste. Collectibles are not liquid. In order to achieve a maximum return on investment, developing a firm selling plan is important.

If the person inheriting the collection does not have the expertise to evaluate and sell the collection properly, he should seek outside help. Obtain an appraisal of the collection. A good appraiser not only provides values but also can develop a sales plan indicating where to obtain the values that he has assigned. Make certain that the appraiser has high ethical standards. When you pay a professional for an appraisal, ethics dictate that the appraiser be prohibited from buying any object that he has appraised or directing the sale of the appraised objects to his place of business. Since there are no licensing standards for appraisers, many do not practice these strict ethical considerations. You are well advised to find someone who does.

Move slowly. You do not have have to take the first course of action that presents itself. There are many options, including auction, consignment, private sale, or donation. It is your choice. Take time to make a wise one and one that fits your needs.

Why don't most collectors dispose of their collections during their lifetime or leave behind adequate records and a sales plan for the person inheriting the collection? The answer rests in how collectors view their collections. Rarely do they see the collection as an investment. The value of the collection is measured by the joy involved in the collecting, not in the potential for financial gain. They never intend to recover the money they have invested. It is an alien concept to the true collector.

Personally, I plan to amend the adage of "live long enough to be a problem to your children" to "live long enough to leave a big problem for your children." If all goes well, this is what I will do. My collection is growing at such an alarming rate that I simply do not have the time to adequately catalog it. I hope to do it someday, but . . .

My collection is my children's legacy. But if they want to get rich from it, they will have to work for their money. Unless they research the objects and their values, plus develop a multiplicity of sale approaches, they will never receive the best value possible. I want them to gain their inheritance the old-fashioned way, "earn it."

Most collectors have a sadistic streak in them somewhere; I am no exception. Sometimes I am not certain that I want another collector to own my things. They are mine and ought to remain mine. King Tut showed one solution to the problem. He was buried with his collection. What a way to go! I thought about this, but I simply do not have the money to build a pyramid.

I do have one recurring dream. My heirs have invited all my rival Historical Staffordshire collectors to my funeral. High above my grave is suspended a trap-door-bottomed box that holds my entire collection. At a given signal the door opens, and my collection falls to earth. Any pieces the collectors catch they can keep. The rest are broken, destroyed forever. As I said, it's only a dream—a nightmare to my rivals, but I always wake up smiling.

Well, it's time to give my answer to the question I posed earlier: "What's going to happen to your stuff when you die?" I thought and thought. Then I realized how simple the answer really is. After I die, it's not going to be my problem. Who cares? I'm just going to keep on collecting.

Recommended Reading

The purpose of this reading list is twofold: (1) to create a good, basic beginners library for collectibles; and (2) to familiarize you with the major publishers in the collectibles field. A few of the books on this list are out-of-print. You will be able to acquire them from one of the many used book dealers specializing in antiques and collectibles titles.

General Price Guide

Rinker, Harry L. *Warman's Americana & Collectibles*, third edition. Published by Warman Publishing Company: 1987.

Identification of Reproductions and Fakes

Hammond, Dorothy. *Confusing Collectibles: A Guide to the Identification of Contemporary Objects*. Published by Wallace-Homestead Book Company: 1979 (revised edition).

———. *More Confusing Collectibles*, volume II. Published by C. B. P. Publishing Company [Wichita, KS]: 1972.

Reference Library

Barlow, Ronald S. *The Antique Tool Collector's Guide to Value*. Published by Windmill Publishing Company: 1985.

Carnevale, Diane (executive editor). *Collectibles Market Guide & Price Index to Limited Edition Plates, Figurines, Bells, Graphics, Steins, and Dolls*, fifth edition. Published by Collectors' Information Bureau: 1988.

Cunningham, Jo. *The Collector's Encyclopedia of American Dinnerware*. Published by Collector Books: 1982.

Docks, L. R. *American Premium Record Guide: Identification and Value Guide to 1915–1965 78s, 45s, and LPs*, third edition. Published by Books Americana: 1986.

Dolan, Maryanne. *Vintage Clothing: 1880 to 1960: Identification and Value Guide*, second edition. Published by Books Americana: 1987.

Florence, Gene. *The Collector's Encyclopedia of Depression Glass*, eighth edition. Published by Collector Books: 1988.

Foulke, Jan. *8th Blue Book Dolls & Values*. Published by Hobby House Press, Inc.: 1987.

Franklin, Linda Campbell. *Identification and Value Guide: 300 Years of Kitchen Collectibles, 2nd Edition*. Published by Books Americana, Inc.: 1984.

Gibbs, P. J. *Black Collectibles Sold in America*. Published by Collector Books: 1987.

Greenberg, Bruce C. [Edited by Christian F. Rohlfing]. *Greenberg's Guide to Lionel Trains: 1901–1942*, Volumes 1 and 2. Published by Greenberg Publishing Company: 1988.

———. [Edited by Roland LaVoie and Steven H. Kimball]. *Greenberg's Guide to Lionel Trains: 1945–1969*, volume 2. Published by Greenberg Publishing Company: 1988.

Hake, Ted, and Russ King. *Price Guide to Collectible Pin-Back Buttons 1896–1986*. Published by Hake's Americana & Collectibles Press: 1986.

Hake, Ted, and Roger Steckler. *An Illustrated Price Guide to Non-Paper Sports Collectibles*. Published by Hake's Americana & Collectibles Press: 1986.

Henzel, S. Sylvia. *Collectibles Costume Jewelry*, revised edition. Published by Wallace-Homestead Book Company: 1987.

Johnson, David and Betty. *Guide To Old Radios: Pointers, Pictures, and Prices*. Published by Wallace-Homestead Book Company: 1989.

Klug, Ray. *Antique Advertising Encyclopedia* (two volumes). Published by L-W Promotions: volume 1, 1978; volume 2, 1985.

Kovel, Ralph and Terry. *The Kovels' Bottle Price List*, seventh edition. Published by Crown Publishers, Inc.: 1984.

Lemke, Bob, and Dan Albaugh. *Sports Collectors' Digest Baseball Card Price Guide*, second edition. Published by Krause Publications: 1988.

Longest, David. *Character Toys and Collectibles* (two volumes). Published by Collector Books: first series, 1984, second series, 1987.

Lowe, James Lewis. *Standard Postcard Catalog*, second edition. Published by Deltiologists of America (10 Felton Avenue, Ridley Park, PA 19078): 1982.

McNulty, Lyndi Stewart. *Wallace-Homestead Price Guide to Plastic Collectibles*. Published by Wallace-Homestead Book Company: 1987.

O'Brien, Richard. *Collecting Toys: A Collector's Identification and Value Guide*, fourth edition. Published by Books Americana: 1985.

Overstreet, Robert M. *The Official Overstreet Comic Book Price Guide, No. 18*. Published by House of Collectibles: 1988.

Petretti, Allan. *Petretti's Coca-Cola Collectibles Price Guide*, fourth edition. Published by Nostalgia Publications, Inc.: 1988.

Sanders, George, Helen Sanders, and Ralph Roberts. *The Price Guide to Autographs*. Published by Wallace-Homestead Book Company: 1988.

Schiffer, Nancy N. *Costume Jewelry: The Fun of Collecting*. Published by Schiffer Publishing Ltd.: 1988.

Shugart, Cooksey, and Tom Engle. *The Official Price Guide to Watches*, eighth edition. Published by House of Collectibles: 1988.

Smith, Jack H. *Postcard Companion: The Collector's Reference*. Published by Wallace-Homestead Book Company: 1989.

Swedberg, Robert W. and Harriett. *Furniture of the Depression Era: Furniture & Accessories of the 1920's, 1930's, and 1940's*. Published by Collector Books: 1987.

Zawacki, Frank. *Famous Faces: Price Guide and Catalog for Magazine Collectors*. Published by Wallace-Homestead Book Company: 1985.

General Purpose

Editors of House of Collectibles. *The Official Directory To U.S. Flea Markets*, second edition. Published by House of Collectibles: 1988.

Hyman, H. A. *Cash for Your Undiscovered Treasures!* Published by Treasure Hunt Publications: 1986.

Kovel, Ralph and Terry. *Kovels' Guide to Selling Your Antiques & Collectibles*. Published by Crown Publishers, Inc.: 1987.

_____. *The Kovels' Collectors' Source Book*. Published by Crown Publishers, Inc.: 1983.

Manston, Peter B. *Manston's Flea Markets, Antique Fairs, and Auctions of Britain*. Published by Travel Keys (P.O. Box 160691, Sacramento, CA 95816).

Wanted To Buy, second edition. Published by Collector Books: 1988.

Just for the Fun of It

Rinker, Harry L. *The Joy of Collecting with Craven Moore*. Published by Wallace-Homestead Book Company: 1985.

Index